REAL-WORLD SCIENCE AND TECHNOLOGY

Written by **Dr. Zondra Knapp**

Illustrator: **Diane Valko**

Editor: **Joel Kupperstein**

Project Director: **Carolea Williams**

Thanks to all the professionals who donated their time, effort, and expertise contributing to this book.

TABLE OF CONTENTS

THE PURPOSE OF THIS BOOK

As teachers, we know that subject matter presented in the classroom prepares students for life and work in the "real world." Students, however, may fail to see this connection. The purpose of *Real-World Science and Technology* is to make that connection apparent—to demonstrate to students, through motivating hands-on activities, how their learning applies to careers they may choose in the future. Through simulations and explanations of technological devices, this book

- shows students that technology can be fun and exciting.
- exposes students to technology-based careers.
- stimulates students' thinking, problem-solving, and creativity.
- demonstrates technology and underlying scientific principles.

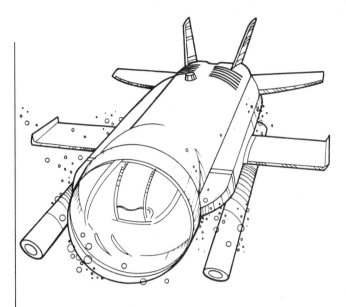

USING THIS BOOK

Whether you are teaching about careers or applying science curriculum to the real world, this book is an excellent resource. Supplement career units with these activities to directly involve students with career tools, or incorporate activities as they naturally fit into your science curriculum. For example, during a unit on sea life, conduct the Submersible activity (pages 33–35) to familiarize students with careers and tools in marine science.

Each activity in the book has five components—a quotation from a professional in a related field, a materials list *(What You Need)*, a procedures list *(What You Do)*, a brief explanation of the activity *(How It Works)*, and extension activities *(Stretching Technology)*. All activities can be reproduced for students and include space for notes and observations. Consider distributing the *How It Works* section after students complete each activity and hypothesize explanations for their results.

Introduce each topic by having students read and discuss the quotation. Brainstorm as a class a list of careers and industries that involve the technology. Then have students research an item from the list to learn about required education, average salary, and job availability in that field. Encourage students to keep a "technology journal" for storing their experiment sheets, recording results, and entering responses to activity questions and *Stretching Technology* topics.

TECHNOLOGY SIMULATIONS

These activities are intended to help students understand how machines work and learn about their applications in the real world. Knowledge of related scientific principles increases with participation in the activities, but the teaching of these principles is a secondary focus of this book. Keep in mind that students must follow directions precisely to create working simulations. Although the activities themselves do not afford students opportunities to freely expand on technological concepts and principles, *Stretching Technology* topics are designed to spark independent discovery and exploration of materials and concepts. Encourage students to investigate at least one *Stretching Technology* topic after completing each activity.

SAFETY AND TECHNOLOGY

These technology experiments require an awareness of safety procedures. The Laboratory Safety Rules (page 5) are guidelines for maintaining safety when working in a technology laboratory. Reproduce and post these rules for student reference during experiments. Make students aware of specific cautions and warnings for each simulation.

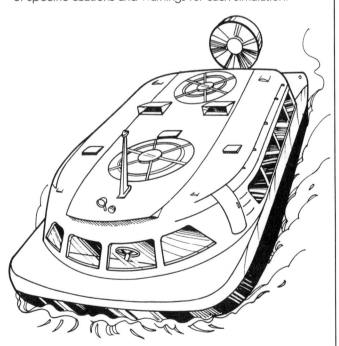

HELPFUL HINTS

The following suggestions will help you organize, prepare, and implement the real-world activities in this book.

- Try all experiments before conducting them with the class. Familiarize yourself with concepts relating to experiments and techniques required to conduct them so you will be prepared to answer questions and solve problems. Decide whether students should work independently, in small groups, or as a whole class.

- Gather materials in advance. To reduce expenses, ask students to donate simple materials such as string, index cards, plastic bottles, and paper clips. On the day of the experiment, display materials on a shelf or table for easy access.

- If possible, invite a guest speaker in a related field to visit the class the day of or the day before the experiment. This will heighten students' interest and eagerness to participate.

- Review applicable safety rules and cautions with students before conducting an experiment.

- Familiarize students with delicate or potentially hazardous materials and tools such as wire cutters, hot plates, diodes, and tin snips before conducting experiments.

- Use the activities as "hooks" or "anticipatory sets" to other units of study to increase student interest and motivation.

- If students are unsuccessful in an activity, invite them to retry the simulation. Reinforce the importance of test-retest reliability in science and technology.

- When applicable, review student journals as a means of authentic assessment. Many *Stretching Technology* topics request journal entries. Have students address these topics as often as possible.

LABORATORY SAFETY RULES

1 Handle nails, saws, wire cutters, and other sharp objects carefully. Always cut objects, poke holes, and strip wires away from your body.

2 Avoid main-line electricity—use low-voltage batteries instead. Keep electrical tools and materials away from water.

3 Wear safety glasses and gloves when working with chemicals, fire, or sharp objects.

4 Maintain close access to water to flush eyes or skin that come in contact with hazardous materials.

5 Avoid wearing loose-fitting clothes, and tie back long hair.

6 Use only recommended amounts of chemicals. Store chemicals in labeled jars with tightly-sealed lids.

7 When working with sound, use caution with increased volume. It may cause damage to eardrums.

8 Avoid looking directly at a light source. It may cause severe eye damage.

9 Know the location of the nearest fire extinguisher and how to use it.

10 Clean spills thoroughly and promptly. Carefully throw away waste.

AIRFOIL

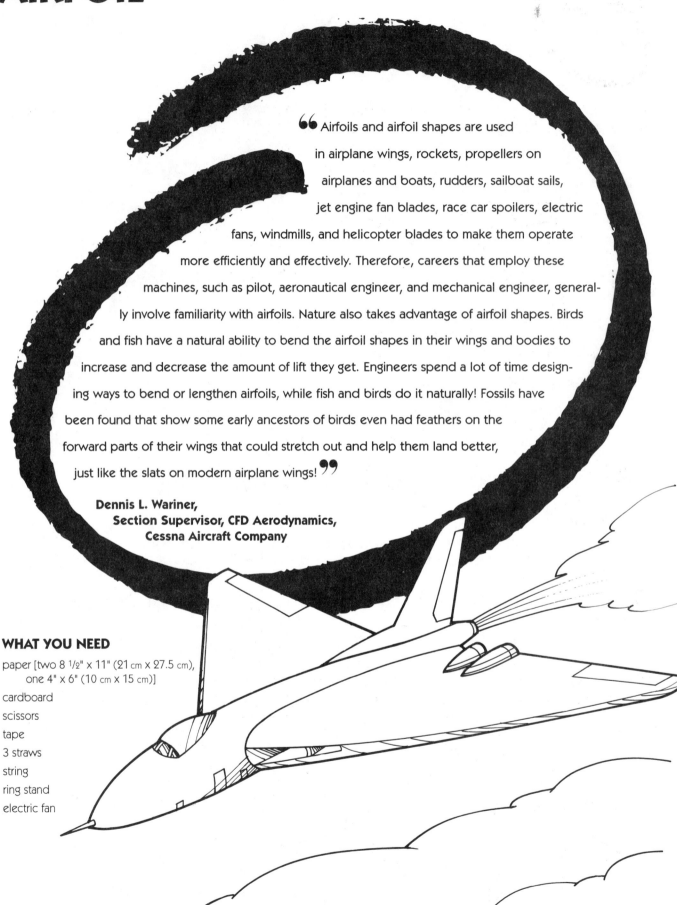

66 Airfoils and airfoil shapes are used in airplane wings, rockets, propellers on airplanes and boats, rudders, sailboat sails, jet engine fan blades, race car spoilers, electric fans, windmills, and helicopter blades to make them operate more efficiently and effectively. Therefore, careers that employ these machines, such as pilot, aeronautical engineer, and mechanical engineer, generally involve familiarity with airfoils. Nature also takes advantage of airfoil shapes. Birds and fish have a natural ability to bend the airfoil shapes in their wings and bodies to increase and decrease the amount of lift they get. Engineers spend a lot of time designing ways to bend or lengthen airfoils, while fish and birds do it naturally! Fossils have been found that show some early ancestors of birds even had feathers on the forward parts of their wings that could stretch out and help them land better, just like the slats on modern airplane wings! 99

**Dennis L. Wariner,
Section Supervisor, CFD Aerodynamics,
Cessna Aircraft Company**

WHAT YOU NEED

paper [two 8 ½" x 11" (21 cm x 27.5 cm),
    one 4" x 6" (10 cm x 15 cm)]
cardboard
scissors
tape
3 straws
string
ring stand
electric fan

1 Fold both 8 ½" x 11" (21 cm x 27.5 cm) papers in half. Tape one edge of each ½" (1 cm) below the other. You will use these to make two different airfoil models.

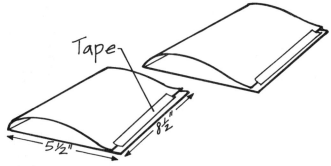

Tape

8 ½"

5 ½"

2 Cut cardboard pieces to fill the gaps in the sides of one "airfoil." Tape the cardboard pieces securely to the sides of the paper.

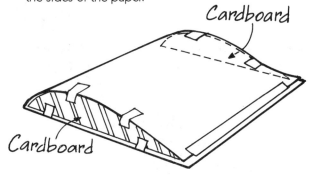

Cardboard

Cardboard

3 Fold the 4" x 6" (10 cm x 15 cm) paper in half. Tape one edge ½" (1 cm) below the other. This is a third airfoil model.

4 Using scissors or a pencil point, poke holes through the top and bottom of each airfoil about 2" (5 cm) behind the curved edge. Run a straw through the holes of each airfoil. Tape the straws to the paper.

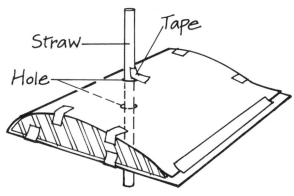

Tape

Straw

Hole

5 Run string through each straw. Wrap the string around the bottom end of each straw and knot it securely, leaving about 6" (15 cm) of string below the knot.

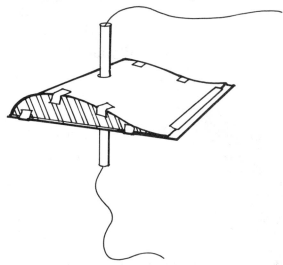

6 Tie the top end of one string to the ring on the ring stand, tape the other end to the base of the stand, and point the folded edge of the airfoil toward the electric fan.

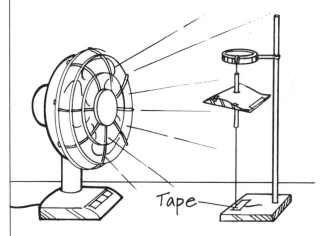

Tape

7 Turn on the fan and observe the airfoil "fly." Turn off the fan and observe what happens to the airfoil.

8 Repeat steps 6 and 7 for the other two airfoils.

9 Record a comparison of the three airfoil models in your technology journal.

HOW IT WORKS

An airplane's wing is flat on the bottom and curved on top like your airfoil models. As a wing moves through the air, the air divides at the front end of an airfoil and recombines at the back. Since the top is curved, air moving over the top has farther to travel and has to move faster than the air underneath in order to recombine. The quicker movement of air above the airfoil creates lower pressure than the slower air below. This difference in pressure causes the airfoil to lift. Varying the size and material composition of the models affects the distribution of air pressure and, as a result, the amount of lift created by the airfoils.

STRETCHING TECHNOLOGY

● Experiment with the size and shape of your airfoils. How do these variables affect their movement? Record results in your technology journal.

● Cut slits and holes in the cardboard of the cardboard-supported airfoil. How does this affect its "flight"?

● Direct the fan at different angles to an airfoil. In your journal, diagram how the angle of the "wind" affects the airfoil's movement.

Notes & Observations

AIRFOIL

Real-World Science and Technology ©1997 Creative Teaching Press

CLOTHES DRYER

Real-World Science and Technology ©1997 Creative Teaching Press

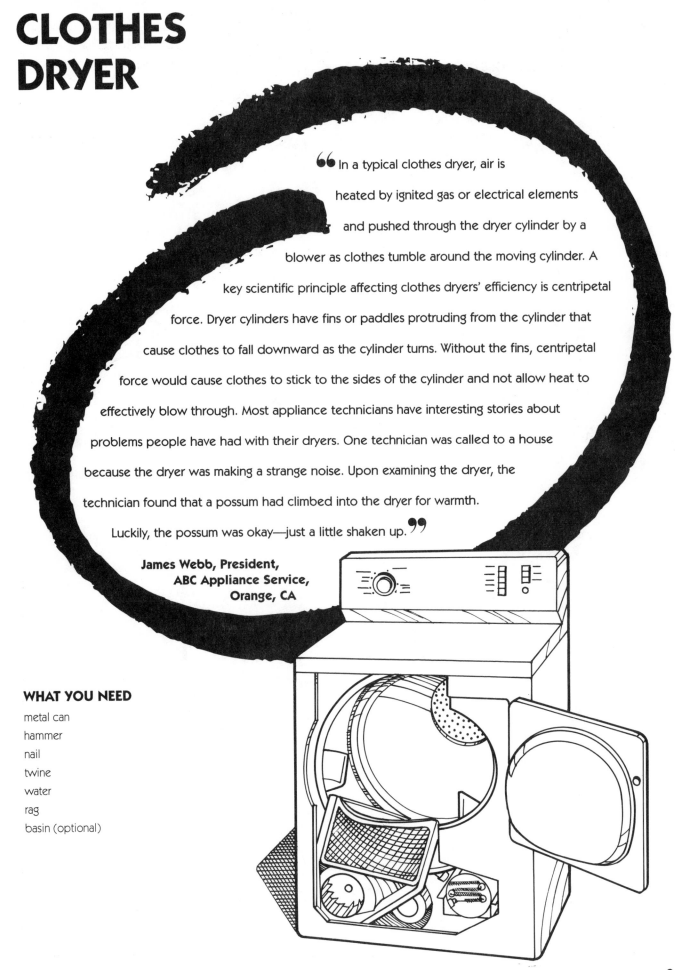

66 In a typical clothes dryer, air is heated by ignited gas or electrical elements and pushed through the dryer cylinder by a blower as clothes tumble around the moving cylinder. A key scientific principle affecting clothes dryers' efficiency is centripetal force. Dryer cylinders have fins or paddles protruding from the cylinder that cause clothes to fall downward as the cylinder turns. Without the fins, centripetal force would cause clothes to stick to the sides of the cylinder and not allow heat to effectively blow through. Most appliance technicians have interesting stories about problems people have had with their dryers. One technician was called to a house because the dryer was making a strange noise. Upon examining the dryer, the technician found that a possum had climbed into the dryer for warmth. Luckily, the possum was okay—just a little shaken up. 99

**James Webb, President,
ABC Appliance Service,
Orange, CA**

WHAT YOU NEED

metal can
hammer
nail
twine
water
rag
basin (optional)

CAUTION: Use care with the hammer and nail.

1 While a partner holds the can against the table, punch holes randomly in the can with the hammer and nail.

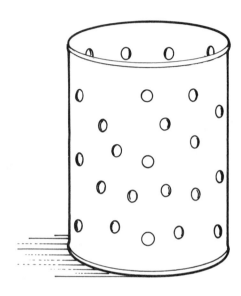

2 Punch three evenly-spaced holes about ½" (1 cm) from the top edge of the can.

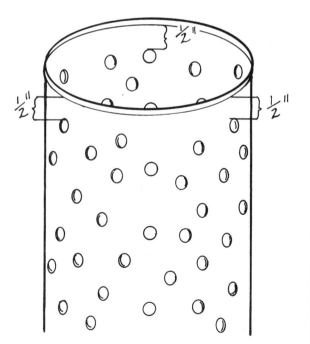

3 Thread and knot a piece of twine through each of these holes. Tie the ends together.

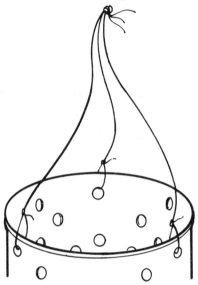

4 Soak the rag in water and put it in the can. (If indoors, hold the can over a basin.)

5 Turn the can around several times, twisting the twine as tightly as possible.

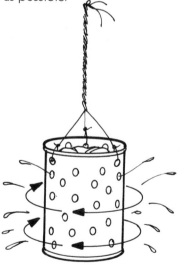

6 Hold the can as far away from your body as possible to avoid getting sprayed. Release the can. Repeat steps 5 and 6 several times.

7 Remove the rag from the can. Is the rag drier than before?

Real-World Science and Technology ©1997 Creative Teaching Press

Once set in motion, an object tends to travel in a straight line. Forces such as gravity and friction change or slow the object's motion. When the can in this experiment spins, it sets the rag and water inside in motion. Centripetal force keeps them from continuing in a straight line. This force is imposed by the can on the rag and water, keeping them pressed against the can's sides and traveling in the same path as the can. Even though moving water escapes through holes in the can, it continues its natural trajectory (a straight line). If the rag were small enough to fit through a hole, it too would fly out of the can. In this activity, unwinding the cords provides the energy to spin the can the way the electric motor spins a real dryer's cylinder.

STRETCHING TECHNOLOGY

● Clothes dryers use heat to accelerate the drying process. In your technology journal, suggest how heat speeds up the process. Then design a way to incorporate heat into your experiment.

● Washers and dryers leave excess dirty water after completing their cycles. In your technology journal, describe and illustrate ways this water can be collected and recycled.

CLOTHES DRYER

Notes & Observations

ELEVATOR

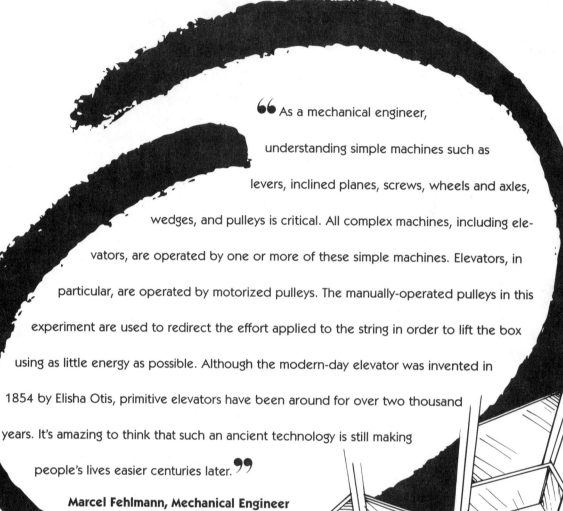

66 As a mechanical engineer,

understanding simple machines such as

levers, inclined planes, screws, wheels and axles,

wedges, and pulleys is critical. All complex machines, including ele-

vators, are operated by one or more of these simple machines. Elevators, in

particular, are operated by motorized pulleys. The manually-operated pulleys in this

experiment are used to redirect the effort applied to the string in order to lift the box

using as little energy as possible. Although the modern-day elevator was invented in

1854 by Elisha Otis, primitive elevators have been around for over two thousand

years. It's amazing to think that such an ancient technology is still making

people's lives easier centuries later. 99

Marcel Fehlmann, Mechanical Engineer

WHAT YOU NEED

hole punch
small box
string
hammer
2 short broad nails
2 shallow metal cans
18" (45 cm) wood board
tape
weight (bag of rocks or marbles)

CAUTION: Use care with the hammer and nails.

1 Punch two holes in a side of the small box. Thread the end of a 70" (175 cm) string in one hole and out the other. Tie the string around the holes.

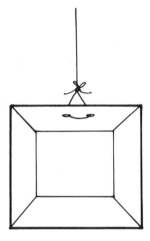

2 Nail a can to each end of the wood board. Be sure the nails go through the center of the cans' bottoms and the cans can turn freely on the nails.

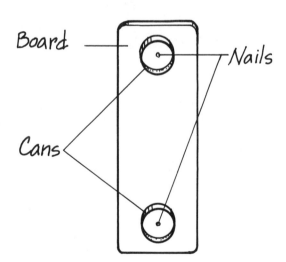

Board — Nails

Cans

3 Place the box on the right side of the board, midway between the two cans so the opening is away from the board and the string is at the top.

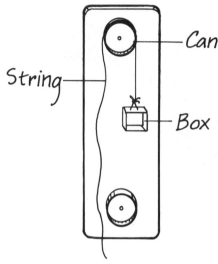

String — Can

Box

4 Run the string around the top can, twice around the bottom can, behind the box, and over the top can again. The string should end on the left side of the board, midway between the cans. Tape down the first loop around the bottom can.

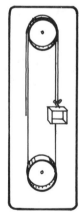

5 Attach the weight to the free end of the string.

6 Stand the board upright. (You may have to lean it against something.) Adjust the amount of weight attached to the string until the box and the weight hang evenly.

7 To operate the elevator, turn the bottom can.

Real-World Science and Technology ©1997 Creative Teaching Press

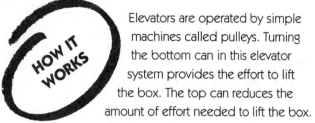

HOW IT WORKS

Elevators are operated by simple machines called pulleys. Turning the bottom can in this elevator system provides the effort to lift the box. The top can reduces the amount of effort needed to lift the box. The weight counterbalances the box in order to prevent gravity from pulling the box down. A real elevator works similarly to this simulation; however, it is turned by an electric motor rather than by hand.

STRETCHING TECHNOLOGY

● Design a way to operate the elevator using the electric generator from page 53 or an electric motor. Draw and label your design in your technology journal.

● How much weight can your elevator lift? Experiment with the amount of string, number of loops around the bottom can, and other variables to maximize your elevator's lifting power.

Notes & Observations

ELEVATOR

Real-World Science and Technology ©1997 Creative Teaching Press

HELICOPTER

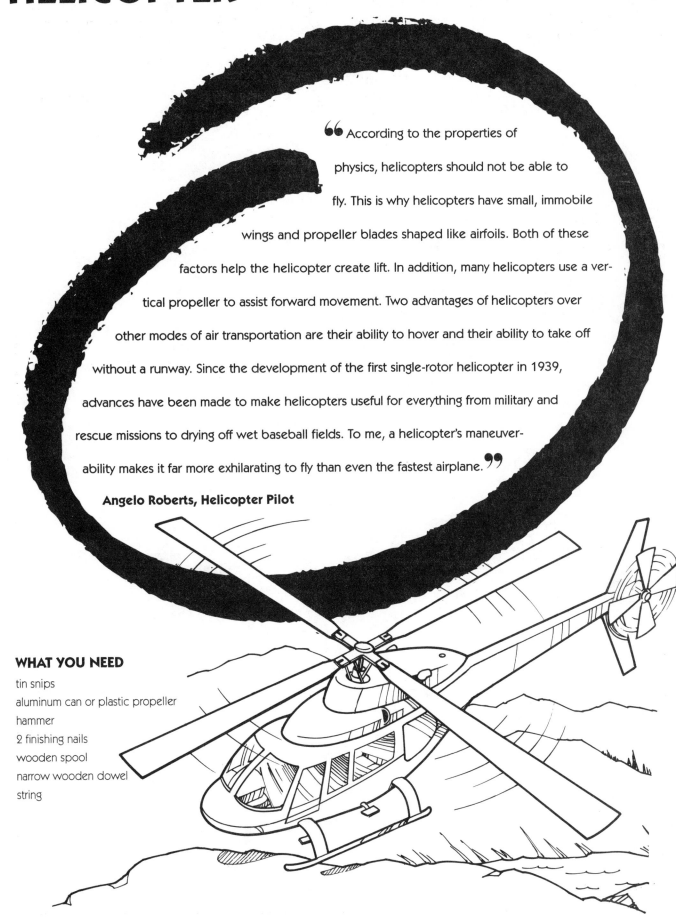

66 According to the properties of physics, helicopters should not be able to fly. This is why helicopters have small, immobile wings and propeller blades shaped like airfoils. Both of these factors help the helicopter create lift. In addition, many helicopters use a vertical propeller to assist forward movement. Two advantages of helicopters over other modes of air transportation are their ability to hover and their ability to take off without a runway. Since the development of the first single-rotor helicopter in 1939, advances have been made to make helicopters useful for everything from military and rescue missions to drying off wet baseball fields. To me, a helicopter's maneuverability makes it far more exhilarating to fly than even the fastest airplane. 99

Angelo Roberts, Helicopter Pilot

WHAT YOU NEED

tin snips
aluminum can or plastic propeller
hammer
2 finishing nails
wooden spool
narrow wooden dowel
string

Real-World Science and Technology ©1997 Creative Teaching Press

CAUTION: Use tin snips, hammer, and nails with care. Wear safety gloves when working with sharp-edged metal.

Note: If you use a plastic propeller, skip steps 1 and 2.

1 Using tin snips, cut a 5" (12 cm) figure-8 from an aluminum can.

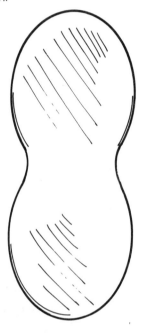

2 Twist the metal in the center so one end faces nearly straight up and the other nearly straight down. Watch for sharp edges!

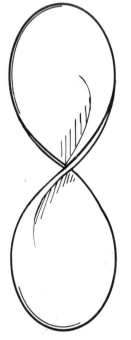

3 Hammer two finishing nails through the metal propeller into the wooden spool. The nails should be on opposite sides of the spool's hole just deep enough so they are not easily moved.

4 Adjust the propeller so it moves freely along the nails.

5 Insert the dowel into the hole in the spool. (Be sure the spool can slide easily off the dowel.) Wrap string around the spool several times.

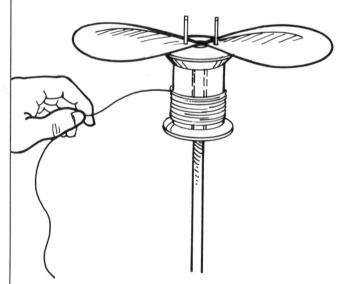

6 In an open area, hold the dowel in one hand and quickly pull the string off the spool with the other. The spinning propeller should lift the spool off the dowel. If the propeller and spool do not fly off the dowel, move the spool closer to the end of the dowel or adjust the amount of string.

Real-World Science and Technology ©1997 Creative Teaching Press

HOW IT WORKS

In a real helicopter, propeller blades spin, blowing air down like a ceiling fan. The force of this air lifts the helicopter off the ground. The blades are curved so they do the work of both a propeller and wings. Tilting the rotor (the shaft that holds the blades) makes the helicopter move in different directions. The blades are bent so they can push air. If blades are straight or facing the same direction, they cut through the air without pushing it in any direction. In this activity, the "helicopter" takes off as air is pushed downward by the spinning propeller blades.

STRETCHING TECHNOLOGY

● Experiment with twisting the propeller blades in different patterns to increase the distance and flight time of your helicopter.

● Redesign your helicopter so it flies in a controlled direction. Sketch the design in your technology journal.

● Research and detail in your technology journal the origin of the word *helicopter*.

Notes & Observations

HELICOPTER

HOVERCRAFT

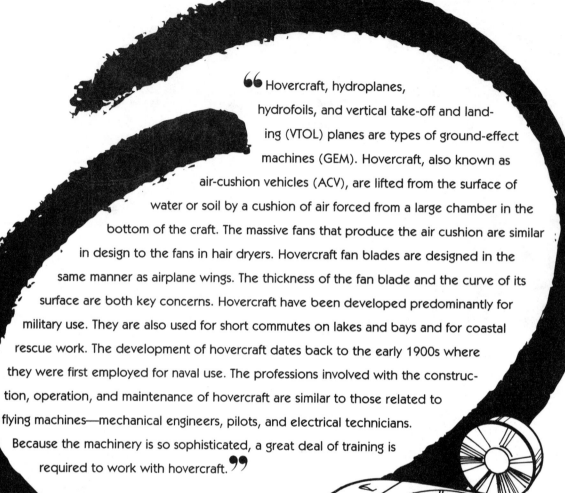

"Hovercraft, hydroplanes, hydrofoils, and vertical take-off and landing (VTOL) planes are types of ground-effect machines (GEM). Hovercraft, also known as air-cushion vehicles (ACV), are lifted from the surface of water or soil by a cushion of air forced from a large chamber in the bottom of the craft. The massive fans that produce the air cushion are similar in design to the fans in hair dryers. Hovercraft fan blades are designed in the same manner as airplane wings. The thickness of the fan blade and the curve of its surface are both key concerns. Hovercraft have been developed predominantly for military use. They are also used for short commutes on lakes and bays and for coastal rescue work. The development of hovercraft dates back to the early 1900s where they were first employed for naval use. The professions involved with the construction, operation, and maintenance of hovercraft are similar to those related to flying machines—mechanical engineers, pilots, and electrical technicians. Because the machinery is so sophisticated, a great deal of training is required to work with hovercraft."

Doug Wolven, Author/Boatbuilder

WHAT YOU NEED

basin
water
scissors
margarine tub lid
one-hole rubber stopper
masking tape
balloon
stopwatch

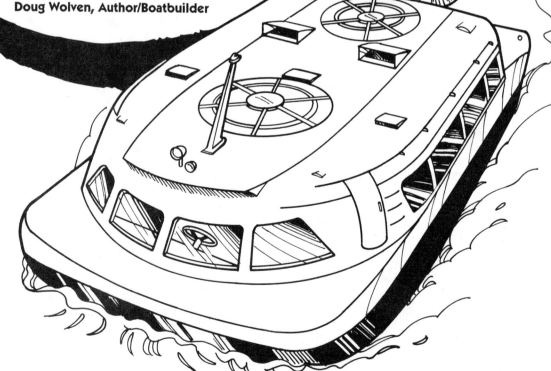

CAUTION: Poke holes away from your body.

1 Fill the basin half full with water.

2 Use a scissor point to poke a hole in the middle of the margarine tub lid.

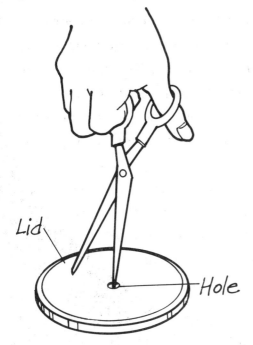

Lid

Hole

3 Line up the hole in the lid with the hole in the rubber stopper and tape the stopper to the top of the lid. Make sure not to cover the hole.

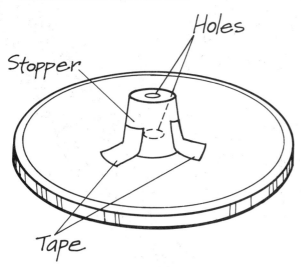

Holes

Stopper

Tape

4 Inflate the balloon. Leaving about half an inch (1 cm) below your fingers, pinch off the balloon. Fit the balloon over the rubber stopper.

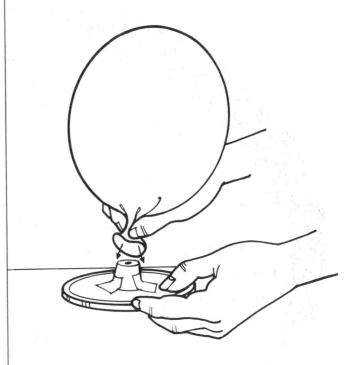

5 Place the hovercraft apparatus in the basin and release your fingers. Time how long it hovers over the surface of the water.

HOW IT WORKS

The force of the air escaping from the balloon causes the "hovercraft" to rise. The weight of the rubber stopper and margarine tub lid keeps it from being propelled out of the basin. In a real hovercraft, air is pumped out by large fans. Since the friction caused by contact with water is removed, hovercrafts travel more smoothly than most boats. This lack of friction also makes it quite energy efficient—less fuel is spent counteracting the resistance of friction. Propellers on a hovercraft's deck blow air out behind the hovercraft to push it forward.

STRETCHING TECHNOLOGY

● Design a way to propel your hovercraft in various directions.

● The damselfly is remarkable because of its ability to hover. Research this insect to find out how it is similar to a hovercraft. Record your findings in your technology journal.

● Try to operate the hovercraft on surfaces other than water. In your journal, list surfaces that work and surfaces that don't. What do the surfaces in each list have in common?

● Attach several lids and balloons side by side to create a more stable craft. In your technology journal, compare the flight length of the larger craft to that of the smaller craft.

Notes & Observations

HOVERCRAFT

Real-World Science and Technology ©1997 Creative Teaching Press

HYDRAULIC PRESS

66 Hydraulic presses operate by applying pressure to a liquid (usually oil) to cause a ram piston to do work such as lifting, moving, and pressing objects. These machines are common tools in manufacturing—particularly in the automotive industry where they are used to manufacture doors, fenders, hoods, and other body parts. Hydraulic presses are also used in the minting of coins, a procedure previously done by hand. The main scientific principle behind the operation of a hydraulic press is the formula $F = PA$, where F is the resulting force, P is the pressure exerted on the oil, and A is the size of the ram piston that exerts the force. This activity does a good job of simulating this principle because it incorporates all the elements of an actual hydraulic press. 99

**Vince Brown, Vice President,
Bay Hydraulics, Inc.**

WHAT YOU NEED

newspaper
two 2-liter plastic bottles
scissors
plastic straw
modeling clay
water
small margarine tub
weight (bag of rocks or marbles)
balloon

1 Cover the work area with newspaper.

2 Cut off the top fourth of the plastic bottles.

3 Using a scissor point, poke a hole about 4" (10 cm) from the bottom in the side of each bottle.

4 Insert an end of the straw into each hole and seal with modeling clay.

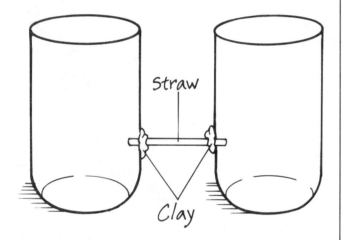

Straw

Clay

5 Pour water into one bottle until the levels in both bottles are 2–3" (5–7 cm) above the straw. (The water should fill the second bottle through the straw.)

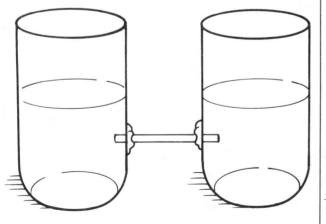

6 Fill the margarine tub with a weight such as a bag of rocks or marbles.

7 Hold the balloon in one bottle and inflate it until it touches the sides. Knot the end securely. Be sure the balloon fits snugly inside the bottle.

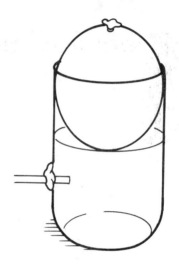

8 Float the weighted tub on the surface of the water in the other bottle.

9 Push down on the balloon until the weighted tub on the other side rises.

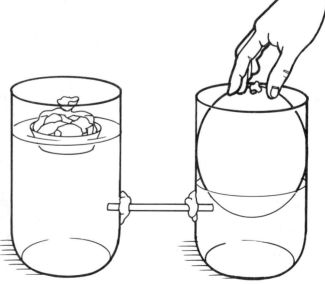

HOW IT WORKS

In this hydraulic press, the pressure applied by the balloon to the water spreads out evenly until it has no place to go but through the straw to the other bottle, pushing the weighted tub upward. The piston in a real hydraulic press works like the balloon in this activity, except it usually uses oil instead of water. The more pressure applied by the piston, the more force exerted on the liquid. Since the weight rises with the liquid, the more pressure applied by the piston, the farther the weight moves.

STRETCHING TECHNOLOGY

● Substitute other liquids for water. Which liquids make the weight easier to lift? Which make it harder to lift? Create a table with this information in your technology journal.

● Research machines that use hydraulic presses. List and describe them in your journal.

● Create a system of measurement to record the force of your hydraulic press by marking the bottle in even increments.

Notes & Observations

HYDRAULIC PRESS

SEISMOGRAPH

"People often think of seismographs as tools for measuring earth-quakes. In fact, seismographs are used to measure any movement of the earth, including nuclear explosions, mining blasts, and movement associated with volcanic activity. Events recorded by seismographs can be used to study the structure of the earth and its layers (the core, mantle, and crust). Seismograms, the recordings produced by seismographs, can be interpreted by seis-mologists and used by engineers to design earthquake-resistant structures such as buildings, highways, and bridges. The information can also be used by civil planners and insurance companies investigating the social response to major earthquakes. Seismographs may seem like a modern technology, but the first device measuring earth movement was invented in 132 A.D. by Chang Heng, a Chinese astronomer and mathematician. Naturally, it wasn't as precise or versatile as a modern seismograph, but it observed the same phenomena."

Diane dePolo, Network Seismologist,
University of Nevada, Reno

WHAT YOU NEED

scissors
construction paper
modeling clay
6" (15 cm) dowel [approx. 1/2" (1 cm)-diameter]
glue
30 plastic bottle caps
large marble

Real-World Science and Technology ©1997 Creative Teaching Press

WHAT YOU DO

1 Cut out a 5" (12.5 cm) construction-paper square.

2 Press a ball of clay onto the center of the paper.

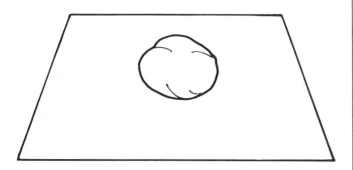

3 Stand the dowel straight up in the center of the clay.

4 Glue plastic bottle caps open-end-up in a circle around the clay. Glue caps in two more concentric circles around the first.

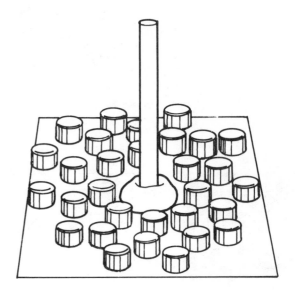

5 Place the marble on top of the dowel. Push against the edge of the table so the marble falls into the first circle of bottle caps. This is a 1 on your version of the Richter scale.

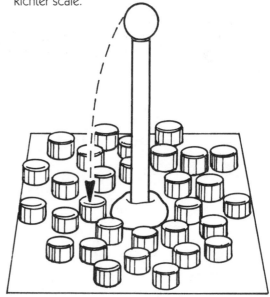

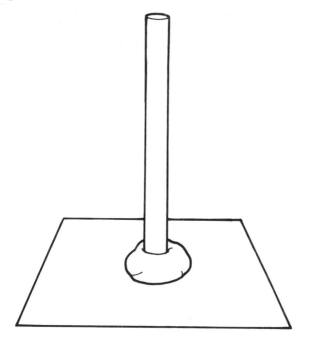

6 Push the table harder and observe where the marble falls. If it lands in the second circle, it is a 2 on the scale; if it lands in the third circle, it is a 3.

HOW IT WORKS

A seismograph is an instrument that amplifies, measures, and records movements of the ground, such as those during earthquakes. These measurements are made on the Richter scale, a scale that indicates an earthquake's intensity. Each increment on the scale indicates a tenfold increase in intensity. For example, a 5 on the Richter scale is ten times stronger than a 4 and 100 times stronger than a 3. In this activity, the movement of the table simulates movement of the earth. The marble on the dowel falls in the direction of the push, just the way the earth's plates move in response to an earthquake. With seismographic records, scientists can find the force and location of the movement. In a real seismograph, the movement of a free weight measures earthquakes—in this simulation, the marble serves the same purpose.

STRETCHING TECHNOLOGY

● Compare your setup with classmates'. Are your bottle caps arranged exactly the same way? Modify your setup to create a standardized measuring tool.

● Research how the Richter scale measures the energy of an earthquake. Write your findings in your technology journal.

● Research the construction of a real seismograph. In your technology journal, compare and contrast it to your simulation.

Notes & Observations

SEISMOGRAPH

Real-World Science and Technology ©1997 Creative Teaching Press

SOUNDPROOFING

66 The most effective soundproof rooms are designed using a combination of three basic principles—to completely contain sound using hard, thick materials; to absorb sound using soft, porous materials; and to diffuse sound using odd-shaped surfaces such as egg cartons. In the recording industry, soundproofing serves two purposes. The first is to contain sound so it does not leak into other areas, and the second is to control acoustics so sounds captured by microphones are as close a representation of original sound as possible. Other occupations and workplaces that use soundproofing are factories that use soundproof walls to contain the sound of loud equipment to prevent damage to workers' ears, schools with soundproof rehearsal facilities, theaters and auditoriums that use soundproofing to assure that audiences can hear precisely what is happening on the stage or screen, and audiologists' booths that use a totally soundproof environment to conduct precise hearing tests. 99

**Tim Keenan, Operations Director,
Creative Media Recording**

WHAT YOU NEED

2 large boxes with lids
glue
egg cartons
heavy fabric
scissors
noisy toy or alarm clock
tape

1 Line one box and lid by gluing egg cartons to all interior sides.

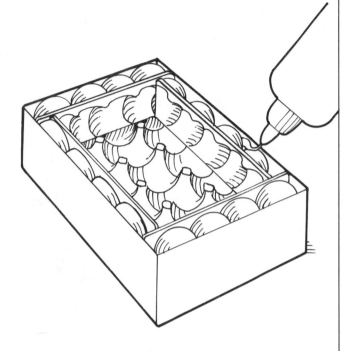

2 Cut fabric to fit the sides and lid of the box. Glue it on top of the egg cartons.

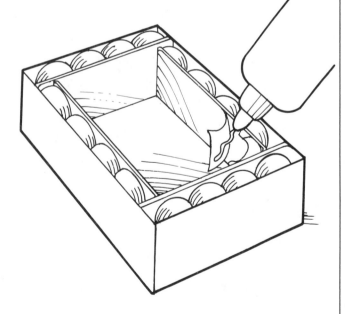

3 Turn on and listen to the noisy toy or alarm clock. Place the toy or clock inside the unlined box, turn it on, replace the lid, and listen to the noise. How much does the unlined box muffle the noise?

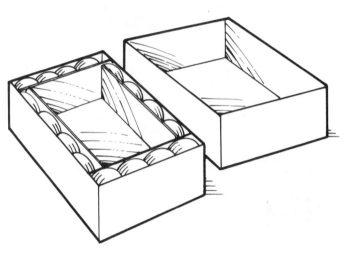

4 Place the toy or clock inside the lined box and tape the lid closed. How much quieter is the toy or clock now that it is inside the box? How effectively did you soundproof the box?

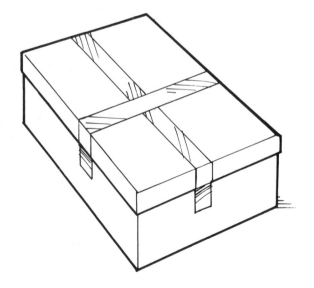

Real-World Science and Technology ©1997 Creative Teaching Press

HOW IT WORKS

Sound travels in waves that become weaker as they move farther from their source or reflect off surfaces. Flat, smooth, hard surfaces efficiently reflect sounds back toward their sources without significantly lessening the strength, causing an echo. Because reflection causes sound waves to weaken, repeated reflection off the sides of the egg cartons in the soundproof "room" causes the strength of the sound to dissipate. In addition, the soft, porous surface of the fabric absorbs sound. The more rough and uneven the surface of the walls and ceiling, the more sound is absorbed.

STRETCHING TECHNOLOGY

● In your technology journal, draw your setup and describe the assembly and results of your soundproofing experiment.

● In your technology journal, list places where soundproofing is beneficial and places where reverberation (echo) is beneficial.

● Brainstorm materials and methods that might improve your soundproof room. (Try boxes of different sizes and thickness, plaster, wood paneling, carpet squares, felt, and soft wallboard.) Test your hypothesis by building a new room.

● Obtain a sound-level meter to measure the amount of noise escaping from each box. The meter will give you an objective measurement of how well your design works.

Notes & Observations

SOUNDPROOFING

STEAM TURBINE

66 The most common places
to find steam turbines are power plants.
Any power plant that uses fuel, whether it's
nuclear, coal, or gas, does so to heat water to create the
steam that powers these turbines. Only power plants using solar,
hydroelectric, and wind power can generate electricity without steam turbines. And even wind turbine generators operate under the same principle as
steam turbines. As an engineer in a power plant, my job is to design ways to make
steam turbines more efficient, so they can generate a maximum amount of electricity
using a minimum amount of fuel. Other engineers in my field are exploring ways to
make fuel-burning power plants more environment-friendly by reducing pollution.
Because nearly all the electricity we use comes from the steam turbines in
fuel-burning power plants, we must find ways to make these plants
cleaner and safer for the environment. 99

Anna Chung, Electrical Engineer

WHAT YOU NEED

hammer
nail
empty tin can (one end open)
12" (30 cm) heavy wire
scissors
heavy-duty aluminum foil
modeling clay
fine mesh square
ring stand
Erlenmeyer flask
water
hot plate

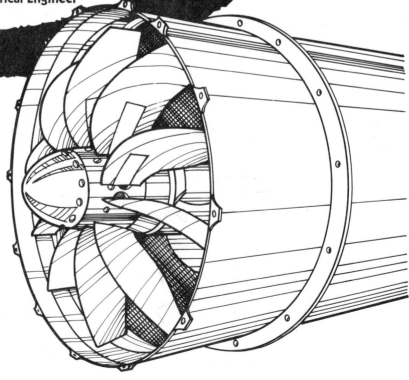

Real World Science and Technology ©1997 Creative Teaching Press

WHAT YOU DO

CAUTION: Do not touch the hot plate when it is on. The flask will become hot when water boils. Let cool before disassembling. Wear safety goggles and tie back long hair. Use care when hammering.

1 Using a nail, hammer two holes 1–2" (2.5–5 cm) apart in the center of the closed end of the can. (The holes should be the same diameter as the heavy wire.)

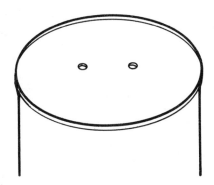

2 Cut a foil circle the same diameter as the can. Poke a small hole in the middle of the circle.

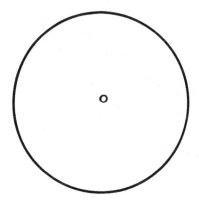

3 Make a pinwheel by cutting six evenly-spaced slits in the foil and twisting the sections in the same direction.

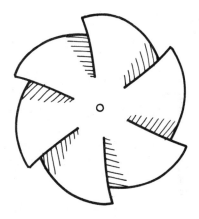

4 Bend 2" (5 cm) of the wire into a right angle, and insert the bent end into the pinwheel. (The pinwheel should turn freely when you blow on it.) Fix the other end in one of the can's holes with modeling clay. Align the pinwheel over the other hole.

5 Place the mesh square on the ring stand, and set the can and pinwheel on top.

6 Fill the flask half full with water. Place it on the hot plate directly below the can and heat to boiling. When steam rises from the boiling water, the pinwheel should turn.

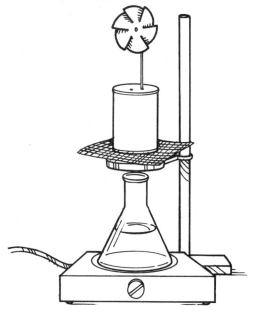

HOW IT WORKS

In a real steam turbine, steam under high pressure turns huge turbine wheels which drive electric generators. In this simulation, when the water boils, the resulting steam is forced through the open hole in the can. Since much less steam can escape through the small hole than is created by the boiling water, pressure builds up, forcing the steam through the hole with enough energy to turn the pinwheel. The narrow diameter of the hole also helps direct the steam toward the pinwheel. A larger hole would allow the steam to flow more slowly and disperse before reaching the pinwheel.

STRETCHING TECHNOLOGY

● Design a way to have your turbine do work. Sketch your design in your technology journal. (Hint: Use the mechanical energy of the pinwheel to spin a magnet near a wire coil. This will create an electric current.)

● Design a turbine that has a larger capacity for work.

● Design multiple turbines that work in tandem.

Notes & Observations

STEAM TURBINE

Real-World Science and Technology ©1997 Creative Teaching Press

SUBMERSIBLE

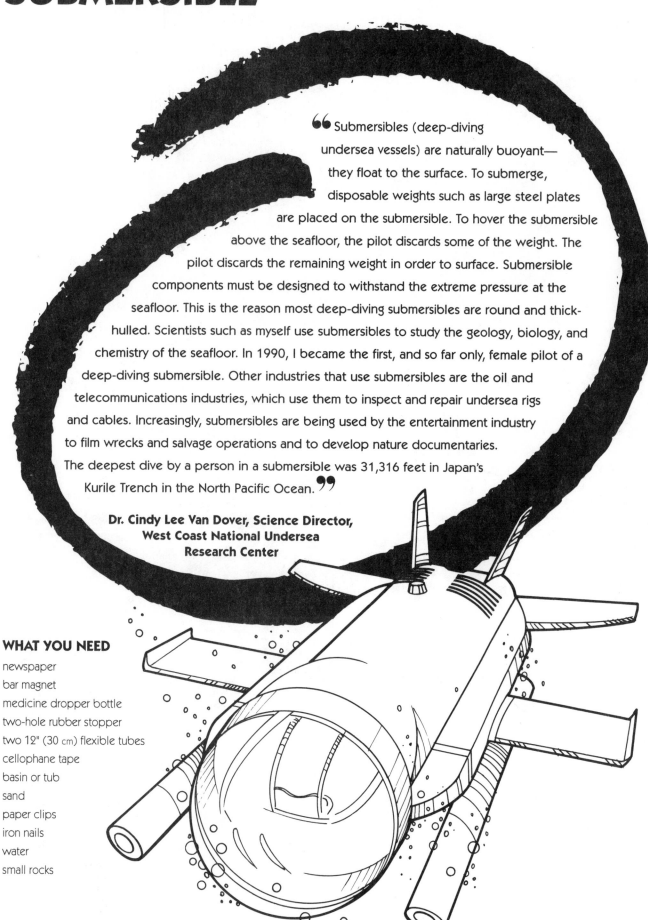

66 Submersibles (deep-diving undersea vessels) are naturally buoyant—they float to the surface. To submerge, disposable weights such as large steel plates are placed on the submersible. To hover the submersible above the seafloor, the pilot discards some of the weight. The pilot discards the remaining weight in order to surface. Submersible components must be designed to withstand the extreme pressure at the seafloor. This is the reason most deep-diving submersibles are round and thick-hulled. Scientists such as myself use submersibles to study the geology, biology, and chemistry of the seafloor. In 1990, I became the first, and so far only, female pilot of a deep-diving submersible. Other industries that use submersibles are the oil and telecommunications industries, which use them to inspect and repair undersea rigs and cables. Increasingly, submersibles are being used by the entertainment industry to film wrecks and salvage operations and to develop nature documentaries. The deepest dive by a person in a submersible was 31,316 feet in Japan's Kurile Trench in the North Pacific Ocean. 99

**Dr. Cindy Lee Van Dover, Science Director,
West Coast National Undersea
Research Center**

WHAT YOU NEED

newspaper
bar magnet
medicine dropper bottle
two-hole rubber stopper
two 12" (30 cm) flexible tubes
cellophane tape
basin or tub
sand
paper clips
iron nails
water
small rocks

1 Cover the work area with newspaper.

2 Place the bar magnet in the bottle and insert the stopper. Insert a tube in each hole of the stopper.

3 Tape the first tube in a U-shaped curve against the outside of the bottle. Adjust the other tube so one end sticks straight up from the bottle and the other emerges just below the bottom of the stopper.

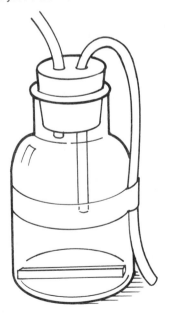

4 Cover the bottom of the basin with sand. Bury paper clips and iron nails in the sand. Slowly fill the basin by running water down one side until three-fourths full.

5 Hold the "submersible" (medicine dropper bottle) in the water. (Be sure no water enters the bottle.) Remove the stopper and place small rocks in the bottle to weigh it down until it sinks slightly below the water's surface. Replace the stopper.

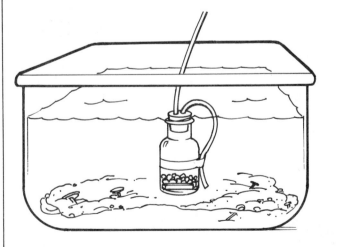

6 Suck air slowly through the tube extending out of the water until the submersible reaches the bottom. Try to pick up nails and paper clips with the magnet. To surface the submersible, blow air into the tube.

Real-World Science and Technology ©1997 Creative Teaching Press

HOW IT WORKS

To submerge, the submersible must be more dense (heavier) than water. Sucking on the tube in your submersible removes air from and draws water into the bottle, making it more dense. To surface, the submersible releases water it has taken in to make it less dense (lighter) than water. Blowing air into the tube replaces the water with air, making the submersible less dense than water and enabling it to surface. In your submersible, the nails and paper clips can be picked up because they are attracted to the magnet in the bottom of the bottle. Many real submersibles use vacuum tubes to collect samples.

STRETCHING TECHNOLOGY

● The more streamlined the design, the less energy required to make the submersible submerge and surface. Use different materials to design a hull to make your submersible more streamlined. How do different designs and materials affect submergibility?

● Compare and contrast a deep-diving submersible with a submarine. Consider their uses, structure, and operation.

Notes & Observations

SUBMERSIBLE

THEODOLITE

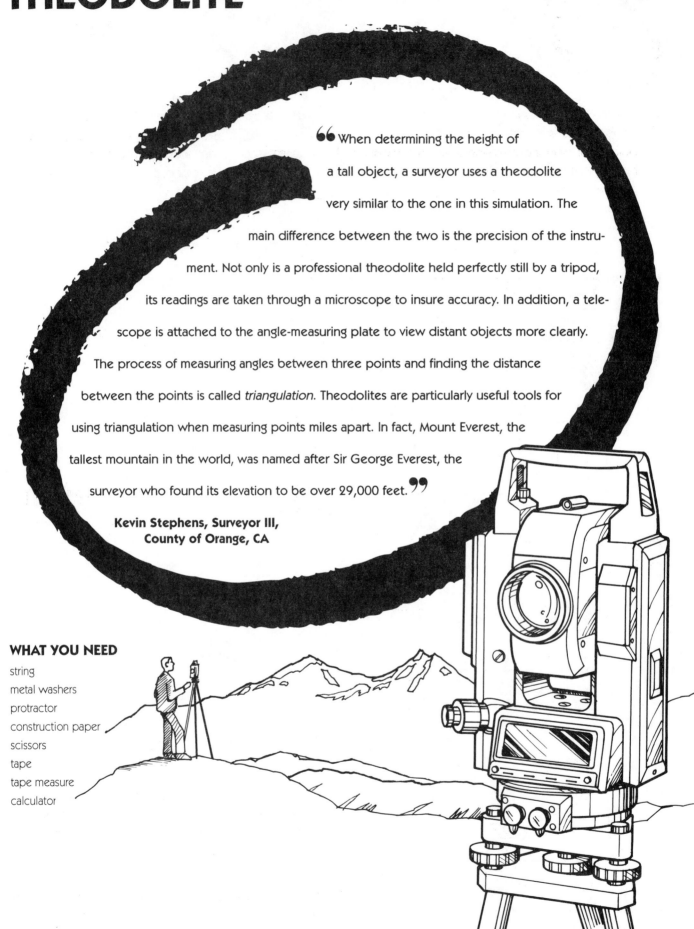

❝ When determining the height of a tall object, a surveyor uses a theodolite very similar to the one in this simulation. The main difference between the two is the precision of the instrument. Not only is a professional theodolite held perfectly still by a tripod, its readings are taken through a microscope to insure accuracy. In addition, a telescope is attached to the angle-measuring plate to view distant objects more clearly. The process of measuring angles between three points and finding the distance between the points is called *triangulation*. Theodolites are particularly useful tools for using triangulation when measuring points miles apart. In fact, Mount Everest, the tallest mountain in the world, was named after Sir George Everest, the surveyor who found its elevation to be over 29,000 feet. ❞

**Kevin Stephens, Surveyor III,
County of Orange, CA**

WHAT YOU NEED

string
metal washers
protractor
construction paper
scissors
tape
tape measure
calculator

WHAT YOU DO

1 Tie one end of a piece of string around several washers and the other through the hole in the protractor. Hold the protractor curved side down so the washers hang along the 90° mark. The washers should hang just below the curved edge.

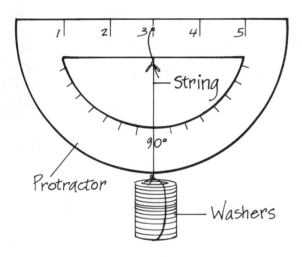

Protractor

String

90°

Washers

2 Make sights by taping a 1" x 4" (2.5 cm x 10 cm) construction-paper strip in a loop to each end of the protractor's straight edge.

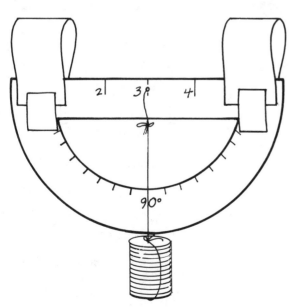

90°

3 Look through the sight loops at a tall object. Press the string against the protractor and read the angle measurement. This is the measurement of the angle at the intersection of the ground and the imaginary line between you and the top of the object. Record this measurement.

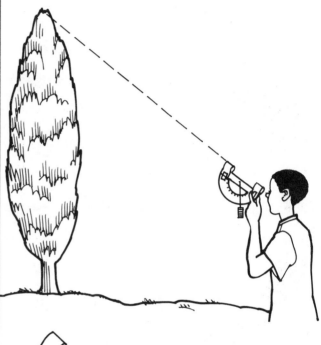

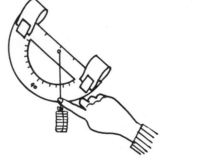

4 Measure and record the distance from where you read the angle to the object itself.

5 Use a calculator or the tangent chart (page 38) to find the tangent (ratio of the side opposite the angle to the side adjacent to the angle) of the angle from step 3. Record this value.

6 Find the height of the object by multiplying the tangent (step 5) by the distance (step 4).

TANGENT CHART

angle	tangent	angle	tangent	angle	tangent	angle	tangent
0°	.0000	23°	.4245	46°	1.0355	69°	2.6051
1°	.0175	24°	.4452	47°	1.0724	70°	2.7475
2°	.0349	25°	.4663	48°	1.1106	71°	2.9042
3°	.0524	26°	.4877	49°	1.1504	72°	3.0777
4°	.0699	27°	.5095	50°	1.1918	73°	3.2709
5°	.0875	28°	.5317	51°	1.2349	74°	3.4874
6°	.1051	29°	.5543	52°	1.2799	75°	3.7321
7°	.1228	30°	.5774	53°	1.3270	76°	4.0108
8°	.1405	31°	.6009	54°	1.3764	77°	4.3315
9°	.1584	32°	.6249	55°	1.4281	78°	4.7046
10°	.1763	33°	.6494	56°	1.4826	79°	5.1446
11°	.1944	34°	.6745	57°	1.5399	80°	5.6713
12°	.2126	35°	.7002	58°	1.6003	81°	6.3138
13°	.2309	36°	.7265	59°	1.6643	82°	7.1154
14°	.2493	37°	.7536	60°	1.7321	83°	8.1443
15°	.2679	38°	.7813	61°	1.8040	84°	9.5144
16°	.2867	39°	.8098	62°	1.8807	85°	11.4301
17°	.3057	40°	.8391	63°	1.9626	86°	14.3007
18°	.3249	41°	.8693	64°	2.0503	87°	19.0811
19°	.3443	42°	.9004	65°	2.1445	88°	28.6363
20°	.3640	43°	.9325	66°	2.2460	89°	57.2900
21°	.3839	44°	.9657	67°	2.3559	90°	∞
22°	.4040	45°	1.0000	68°	2.4751		

In a real theodolite, the plumb line (string or wire with a weight at the end) measures the angle at each end of the horizontal line of an imaginary right triangle. This mathematical calculation is called *triangulation*. Surveyors use triangulation to measure distances for building roads, highways, and tall buildings. Surveyors can find the height of any building—from a small house to the tallest skyscraper—using a theodolite. Theodolites called *astrolabes* were used by sailors for navigation and measuring distances between stars.

● Tie the end of a 3–6' (1–2 m) piece of string around a paper clip. Mold clay around the paper clip. Hang the string (*plumb line*) along a door post or windowsill. Is the structure perfectly vertical? Does it lean inward or outward? Brainstorm other uses for plumb lines.

● Design a way to make your theodolite more stable and accurate. (Hint: Try to simulate components of a real theodolite that improve its precision.)

Notes & Observations

THEODOLITE

WIND TUNNEL

66 In industry as well as scientific research, wind tunnels are used to test the lift of airplane wings and other similarly-shaped bodies. Inside the wind tunnel, the speed of the air blown over the wing is increased until the maximum amount of lift for that wing shape is found. Interestingly, car designers use wind tunnels for exactly the opposite reason that airplane designers use them. While airplane designers try to maximize how well wind lifts a plane, car designers try to maximize how well wind pushes down a car. This is because the harder a car presses against the road, the better its handling will be. In addition, cars and planes with aerodynamic designs receive little wind resistance, enabling them to improve their fuel efficiency. 99

Michael Gran, Aerospace Engineer

WHAT YOU NEED

plastic straws
string
fine mesh netting
scissors
milk carton
stapler
ribbon
electric fan
airfoil (pages 6–8)
tape
modeling clay
pan balance
gram and kilogram weights

WHAT YOU DO

1 Tie a large bundle of plastic straws together with string.

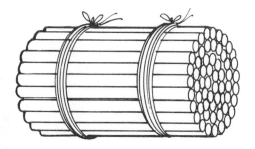

2 Wrap the bundle in fine mesh netting.

3 Cut out the ends of the milk carton. Place the bundle inside the carton and staple the netting to the corners. Cut the carton to the same length as the straws.

4 Staple a 12" (30 cm) ribbon to each corner of one side of the carton. Point the electric fan so it faces the side of the carton without the ribbon.

5 Pierce a hole through the bottom of the airfoil about 3" (7.5 cm) behind the fold and push a straw through the hole. Securely tape the straw to the top of the airfoil.

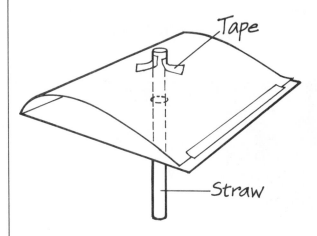
Tape
Straw

6 Stand the airfoil in a modeling clay base.

7 Place the airfoil on one side of a pan balance with the curved edge pointing toward the wind tunnel.

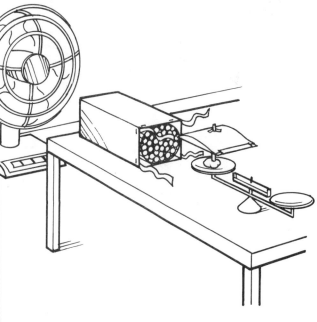

8 Turn on the fan. Add weights to the pan balance until both sides are even. This weight measures the amount of force needed to lift the airfoil.

Engineers use wind tunnels to measure how much lift different wing shapes produce and which shapes are best suited for airplanes. In your airfoil, air passes over the wing. The farther air has to travel over the surface of the wing, the faster it has to go, and the lower the air pressure it creates. Lower air pressure above the wing than below it creates lift. In your wind tunnel, air from a fan is blown through a bundle of straws to direct the air stream. The amount of lift on the wing is measured by the weight that keeps the wing balanced.

● Design other kinds of wind tunnels. Experiment with different-sized boxes and straws and other sources of wind.

● Research resistance and lift by finding out how wings of gliders and jet planes differ from airplane wings. Describe the differences in your technology journal.

Notes & Observations

WIND TUNNEL

WIND TURBINE GENERATOR

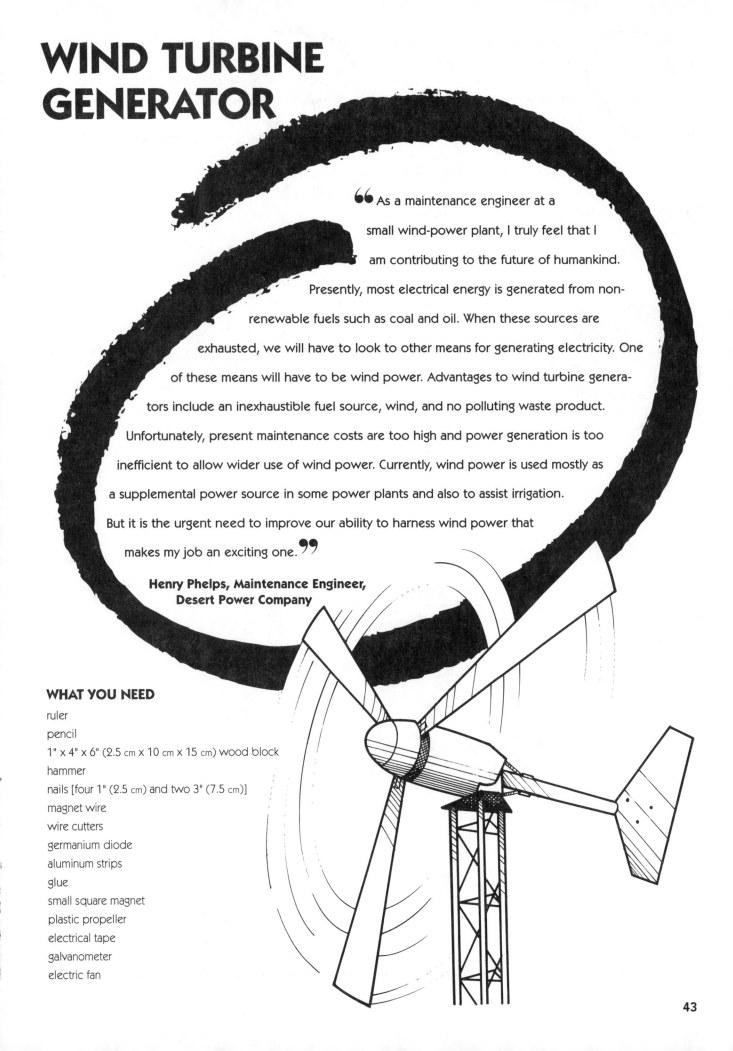

66 As a maintenance engineer at a small wind-power plant, I truly feel that I am contributing to the future of humankind. Presently, most electrical energy is generated from non-renewable fuels such as coal and oil. When these sources are exhausted, we will have to look to other means for generating electricity. One of these means will have to be wind power. Advantages to wind turbine genera-tors include an inexhaustible fuel source, wind, and no polluting waste product. Unfortunately, present maintenance costs are too high and power generation is too inefficient to allow wider use of wind power. Currently, wind power is used mostly as a supplemental power source in some power plants and also to assist irrigation. But it is the urgent need to improve our ability to harness wind power that makes my job an exciting one. 99

**Henry Phelps, Maintenance Engineer,
Desert Power Company**

WHAT YOU NEED

ruler
pencil
1" x 4" x 6" (2.5 cm x 10 cm x 15 cm) wood block
hammer
nails [four 1" (2.5 cm) and two 3" (7.5 cm)]
magnet wire
wire cutters
germanium diode
aluminum strips
glue
small square magnet
plastic propeller
electrical tape
galvanometer
electric fan

CAUTION: Aluminum strips may be sharp—handle carefully. Use hammer and nails with care.

1 Using a ruler, draw a 3" (7.5 cm) triangle on the wood block. Hammer 1" (2.5 cm) nails halfway into the block at the two bottom corners of the triangle parallel to the edge of the block.

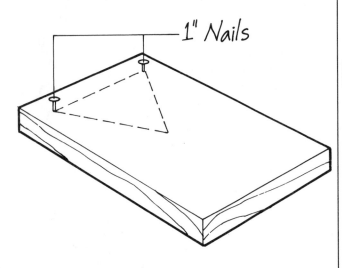

1" Nails

3 Connect the free wire ends to the two 1" (2.5 cm) nails.

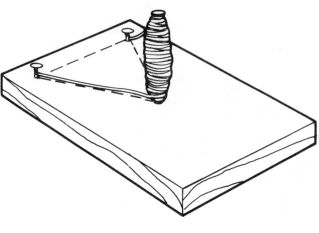

2 Hammer the tip of a 3" (7.5 cm) nail far enough into the top point of the triangle so it is free-standing. Tightly wrap a thick coil of magnet wire around the nail. Leave at least 3" (7.5 cm) of the wire free at each end. Strip the insulation off the wire ends.

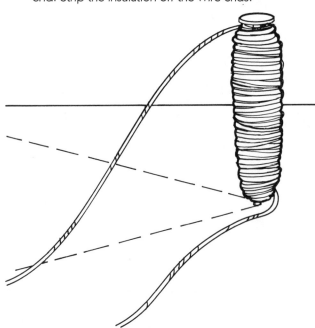

4 Connect the diode between the 1" (2.5 cm) nails.

Diode

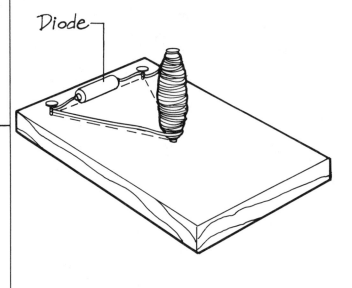

Real-World Science and Technology ©1997 Creative Teaching Press

5 Using a long nail, hammer holes ½" (1 cm) from the top of the aluminum strips. Fold the strips into L shapes and nail them with 1" (2.5 cm) nails to the wood block, aligned with the top of the triangle.

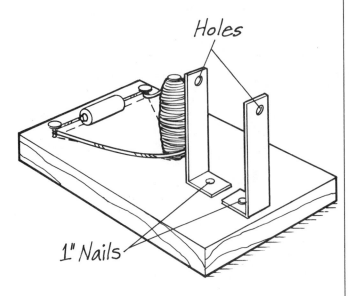

Holes

1" Nails

6 Glue the magnet to the head of a 3" (7.5 cm) nail. Insert the nail through the holes in the aluminum strips, and attach the plastic propeller to the other end. Be sure the magnet is directly over the wire-wound nail. To keep the nail from sliding back and forth, wrap electrical tape around it outside the aluminum strips.

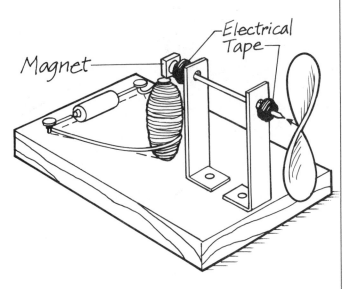

Magnet

Electrical Tape

7 Use wire with stripped ends to attach the galvanometer to the small nails.

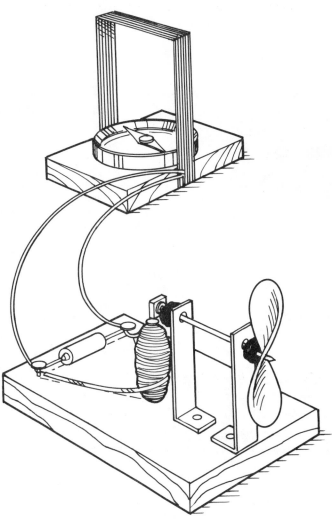

8 Face the propeller toward the electric fan. When the propeller turns, the galvanometer should indicate electricity is being generated.

In your wind turbine, wind turns the propeller and magnet. By a process called *electromagnetic induction*, the spinning magnet generates an alternating current (AC) in the wire wound around the long nail. This current is converted into direct current (DC) by the diode. When the propeller shaft turns, the needle in the galvanometer moves, showing that electricity is generated.

● What other materials can you use to support the propeller shaft?

● Does the generator produce enough energy to light a lightbulb? Design an experiment to find out.

● Wind turbine generators need to be located in places with consistent, strong winds. In your technology journal, list places in your school or neighborhood suitable for a wind turbine generator. If possible, test these places using your generator.

Notes & Observations

WIND TURBINE GENERATOR

Real-World Science and Technology ©1997 Creative Teaching Press

BATTERY

66 When people think of uses for batteries, they usually think of flashlights, portable radios, cameras, and electronic games. But there are many other uses for batteries people rarely consider. For example, exit signs in schools are powered by batteries when electricity is turned off. Boats, campers, cars, trucks, trains, and airplanes use batteries. Telephone companies, electric utilities, and large computer operations use batteries to keep their equipment running non-stop. Military tanks, fighter jets, and submarines use batteries. Wheelchairs and hearing aids use them, too. In many countries, batteries are used in solar-electric systems to provide power to homes, churches, and schools. Batteries are also used to supply energy to refrigerators that store disease-fighting vaccines in remote areas of the world. Engineers are in the process of refining plans for cost-efficient cars and buses powered by electric batteries instead of gasoline. As you can see, there are hundreds of careers that involve batteries—many of them in unexpected ways. 99

**Jim Drizos, Product Applications Manager,
Trojan Battery Company,
Santa Fe Springs, CA**

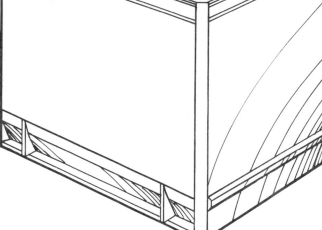

WHAT YOU NEED

6 pennies
steel wool
six 1" (2.5 cm)
    blotting paper squares
lemon juice
six 1" (2.5 cm)
    aluminum foil squares
wire cutters
two 12" (30 cm) insulated wires
electrical tape
lightbulb and socket

WHAT YOU DO

CAUTION: Use wire cutters carefully. Be sure blotter paper is dry before connecting wires. Do not touch exposed parts of the setup when connected.

1 Clean the pennies with steel wool.

2 Soak the blotting paper squares in lemon juice. Press out most of the juice by running your fingers down each piece and pinching the ends.

3 Alternately stack pennies, blotting paper, and foil squares, starting with a penny and ending with a foil square on top.

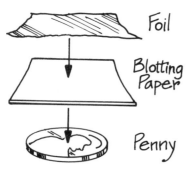

Foil

Blotting Paper

Penny

4 Strip the insulation off the ends of the wires. Tape one wire to the foil on top of the stack and the other to the penny on the bottom. Run tape lengthwise around the stack to hold it together.

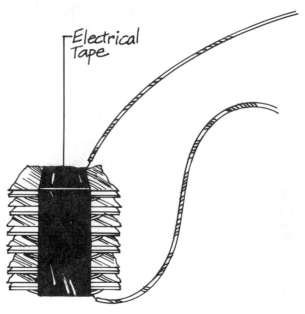

Electrical Tape

5 Connect the loose ends of the wires to the lightbulb socket. The bulb should light.

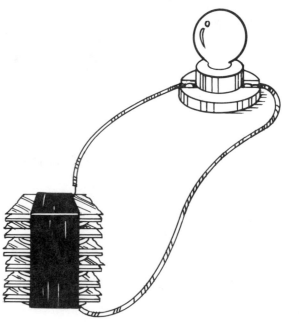

Real-World Science and Technology ©1997 Creative Teaching Press

In your battery, electricity was made by the electrochemical interaction between two metals and an electrolyte (lemon juice). An electrolyte is a substance that produces an electric current when in contact with a conductive metal. In a real battery, the case is made of zinc covered with cardboard and plastic or tin. Instead of copper coins, there is a carbon rod in the middle. Real batteries are encased because their electrolytes often consist of strong acids or bases. As electricity is generated by a battery, the chemicals inside are slowly depleted.

● Find out the maximum wattage lightbulb your battery can light.

● Experiment with different coins, arrangements, sizes, and stack lengths. Design a way to increase the strength of the battery.

● Batteries are classified in different ways. Based on design, batteries are classified as *primary* or *secondary*. Based on composition, batteries are classified as *wet cells* or *dry cells*. Research and describe in your technology journal the differences between these categories. What type of battery did you build in this simulation?

● Use a galvanometer (pages 66–68) to test electric current. Remove the connections to the lightbulb and connect them to the compass. Record any change or movement in the compass needle.

Notes & Observations

BATTERY

COIN-OPERATED MACHINE

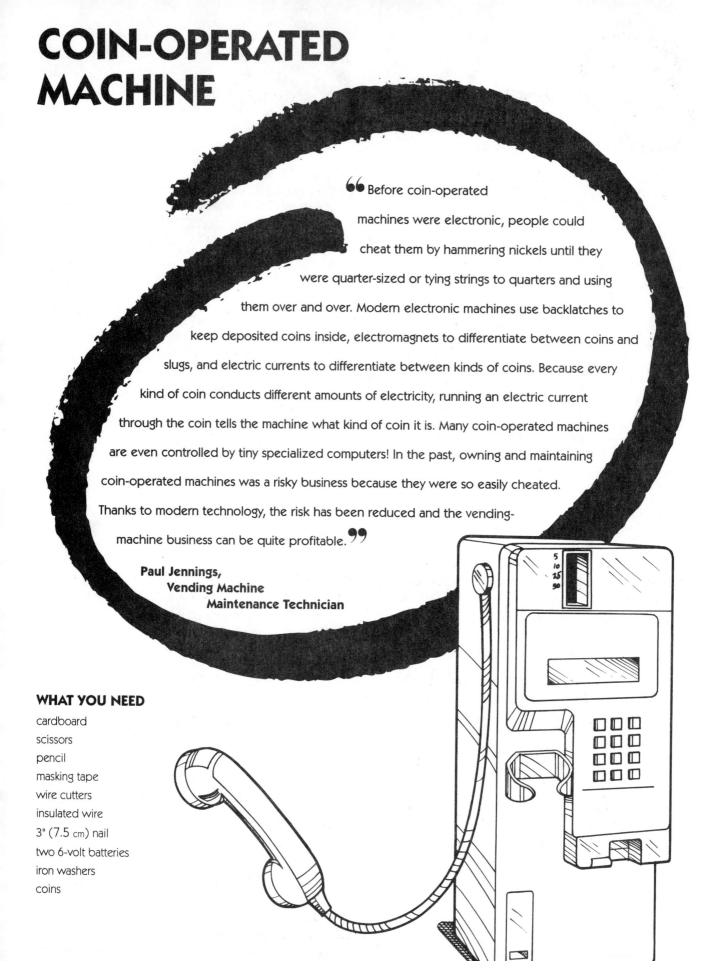

❝Before coin-operated machines were electronic, people could cheat them by hammering nickels until they were quarter-sized or tying strings to quarters and using them over and over. Modern electronic machines use backlatches to keep deposited coins inside, electromagnets to differentiate between coins and slugs, and electric currents to differentiate between kinds of coins. Because every kind of coin conducts different amounts of electricity, running an electric current through the coin tells the machine what kind of coin it is. Many coin-operated machines are even controlled by tiny specialized computers! In the past, owning and maintaining coin-operated machines was a risky business because they were so easily cheated. Thanks to modern technology, the risk has been reduced and the vending-machine business can be quite profitable.❞

Paul Jennings,
Vending Machine
Maintenance Technician

WHAT YOU NEED

cardboard
scissors
pencil
masking tape
wire cutters
insulated wire
3" (7.5 cm) nail
two 6-volt batteries
iron washers
coins

Real-World Science and Technology ©1997 Creative Teaching Press

CAUTION: Do not touch bare wire in a complete circuit.

1 Cut a 9" x 24" (22.5 cm x 60 cm) cardboard piece. Fold it into a V shape so it stands freely.

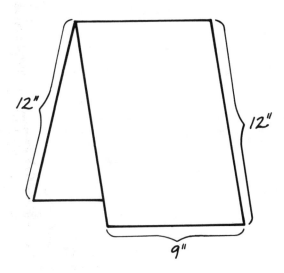

12" 12"

9"

2 Draw a line down the middle of one side of the V. Label the left side *rejected* and the right side *accepted*. Tape a wire-wrapped nail to the left of the line. Strip the insulation off each end of the wire.

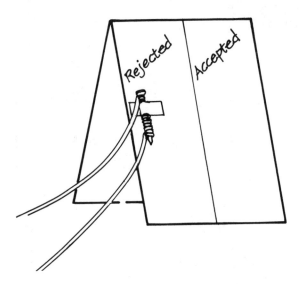

3 Attach the ends of the wire coming off the nail to two batteries connected in a series circuit.

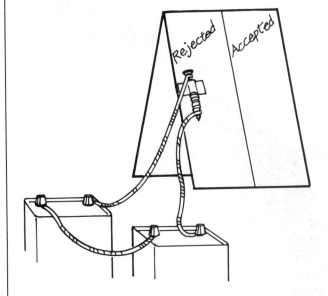

4 At the center of the top of the board, draw a 1 ½" (4 cm) square. This is the "coin slot."

5 Cut a 3" x 12" (7.5 cm x 30 cm) piece of cardboard and fold it into a V shape. Tape it upside down slightly to the left of the middle line of the large cardboard V.

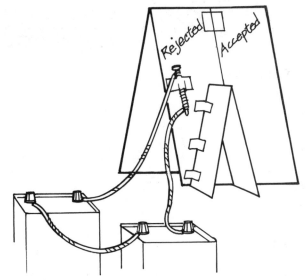

6 Place a coin or washer on the coin slot. Let the coin or washer slide down the line. On which side does it land? Is it magnetic? non-magnetic? Test a variety of coins and "slugs" (counterfeit coins).

HOW IT WORKS

Because iron washers are magnetic, they are drawn toward the electromagnet. Coins are non-magnetic, therefore not attracted to the electromagnet. When released, the coins slide straight down the cardboard, landing in the *accepted* section. A real coin-operated machine uses electric currents to differentiate between coins—it sorts coins by testing the amount of electricity conducted. Since each coin type conducts a different amount of electricity, the machine can identify coins by running electric current through them.

STRETCHING TECHNOLOGY

● The "machine" in this activity can be operated with coins from other countries as well as any other non-magnetic disk. Redesign your machine so it only accepts the correct coins.

● In your technology journal, list instruments, machines, and household appliances that use magnets and electromagnets.

● Pushing a washer or other slug down the center line with great force can make it fall to the *accepted* side. Hypothesize how real coin-operated machines prevent this from happening.

Notes & Observations

COIN-OPERATED MACHINE

Real-World Science and Technology ©1997 Creative Teaching Press

ELECTRIC GENERATOR

66 Electricity is produced in a power plant's generator by rotating a magnetic field across stationary conductors which are connected to form large coils. The electrically-created magnetic field is rotated by a steam or water turbine. In the past, the size of a generator was limited by the tremendous amount of heat given off. Today, electric generators are cooled by water, enabling power companies to build much larger, more powerful generators. Since electricity and water are such a dangerous combination, it may seem strange to have electrical conductors cooled by water, but in fact, water-cooling systems have incited vast improvements in this technology. On a much smaller scale, this simulation is much like a power plant's generator—they both convert mechanical energy to electric energy. The difference is that the simulation derives its mechanical energy from an electric motor, while a real generator derives its mechanical energy from steam or water. 99

**Mike Schuck, Supervising Engineer 4,
Southern California Edison**

WHAT YOU NEED

electrical tape
AA battery
2 small electric motors
lightbulb and socket
shoe box lid
wire cutters
insulated wire
alligator clips
rubber tubing

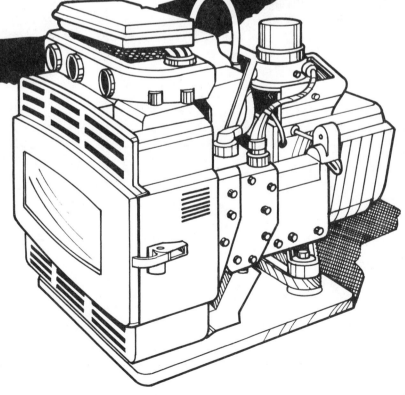

CAUTION: Do not touch bare wire in a complete circuit.

1 Tape the battery, motors, and lightbulb in a row inside the shoe box lid. Point the back of one motor toward the battery and the back of the other toward the lightbulb. The rotors (the spinning parts of the motors) should face each other.

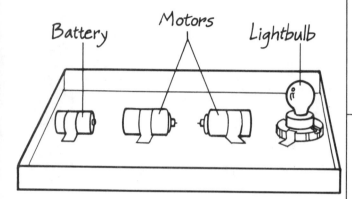

Battery   Motors   Lightbulb

2 Cut four wires approximately 6" (15 cm) long. Strip about 2" (5 cm) of insulation off each end.

3 Connect one end of each of two wires to a battery, and the other ends to the terminals of the first motor. (Use alligator clips to connect the wire and motor.)

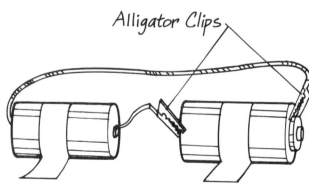

Alligator Clips

4 Connect one end of each of the other two wires to the lightbulb socket, and the other ends to the terminals of the second motor. Again, use alligator clips.

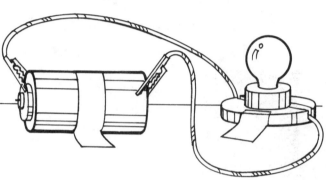

5 Using rubber tubing, attach the spinning rotor of the first motor to the stationary rotor of the second motor. The second motor's rotor should spin, and the bulb should light, even though there is no direct source of electricity.

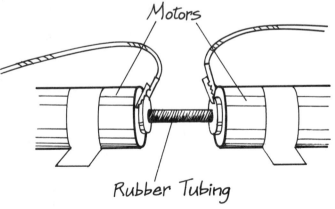

Motors

Rubber Tubing

Real-World Science and Technology ©1997 Creative Teaching Press

HOW IT WORKS

All generators—hydroelectric, nuclear, wind turbine, and hand-crank—convert mechanical energy into electrical energy. In this activity, mechanical energy is provided by the battery-powered motor. The connecting rubber tube causes the second motor to spin. The movement of the second motor causes the magnet inside the motor to rotate inside the motor's coil, creating an electric current. (This is called *induction.*) This electricity is changed to heat and light when it reaches the lightbulb. Even though the two motors are identical, they serve different purposes. The first converts electrical energy into mechanical energy, and the second—the "generator"—converts mechanical energy into electrical energy.

STRETCHING TECHNOLOGY

● Portable generators are handy when electric outlets are unavailable. In your technology journal, list and describe circumstances in which a portable generator would be useful.

● Experiment with different motors, wires, and batteries to light the bulb as brightly as possible. Draw a diagram of your new setups in your technology journal.

● Switch the connections so the battery and lightbulb are reversed. Which motor is now generating electricity?

Notes & Observations

ELECTRIC GENERATOR

ELECTRIC LIGHTBULB

> **Lightbulbs, also referred to as incandescent or filament lamps, are made in a great variety of electrical ratings, physical sizes, and shapes, but all operate on the same principle of light production—a wire is heated to incandescence (glowing) by passing an electric current through it. Thomas Edison brought out the first successful lamp of this type in 1879, and since then, many improvements have been made, particularly in types of filaments and methods of manufacturing. Today, lightbulbs can be found in television lamps, flashbulbs, home lighting, streetlights, germicidal lamps, miner's lamps, and hundreds of other places. Any career, hobby, or chore that involves lighting can be made simpler with an understanding of incandescent bulbs. In this experiment, you will get the same results in less than an hour that Thomas Edison took 18 months and $40,000 to achieve.**

Ernest B. Knapp, Western Regional Sales Manager, Venture Lighting International

WHAT YOU NEED

5" (12.5 cm) nichrome wire
2 nails
hammer
wide-mouth jar and lid
modeling clay or electrical tape
two 8" (20 cm) insulated wires
wire cutters
6-volt battery

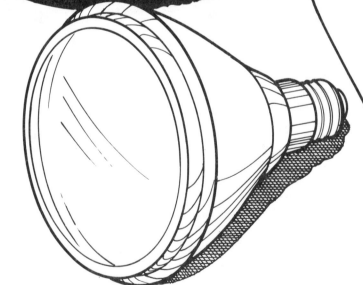
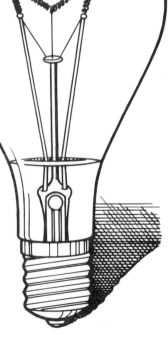

WHAT YOU DO

CAUTION: Do not touch bare wire in a complete circuit. Let the nichrome-wire filament cool before disassembling.

1 Wind the nichrome wire around a nail several times to make a loose coil. Remove the wire from the nail. This is the lightbulb's filament.

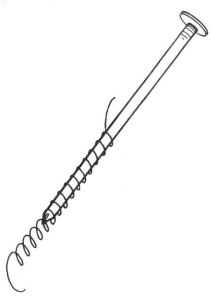

3 Seal the lid on the jar with modeling clay or electrical tape.

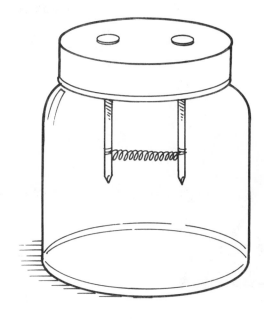

2 Hammer two nails into the jar lid about 2" (5 cm) apart so the nails hang into the jar. Connect the nichrome-wire filament to the ends of the two nails.

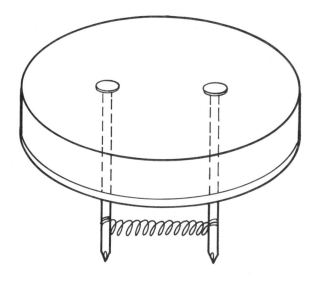

4 Strip the insulation off the ends of the 8" (20 cm) insulated wires, and place an end of each under the head of a nail so it is pressed between the nail head and the jar lid. Attach the free ends of the wires to the battery, and observe the filament. Leave the circuit connected for only a few seconds.

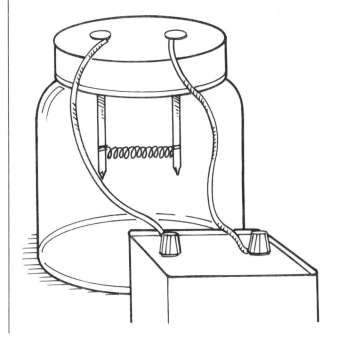

HOW IT WORKS

A real lightbulb operates because the high resistance of thin wire filaments produces heat. Heated metals glow as the temperature increases. Lightbulbs use a coiled filament in a glass enclosure. In this activity, a coil of nichrome wire simulates the filament of an incandescent lightbulb. When you switched on the electricity, your bulb produced heat and light. Manufacturers remove air from lightbulb encasements or replace it with argon or nitrogen so filaments last a long time.

STRETCHING TECHNOLOGY

● Experiment with different kinds of filament wire to see which burn brightest and longest. Record results in your technology journal.

● Evacuate the air in the jar by placing a lit candle inside. Quickly close the lid. When the candle goes out, connect the circuit. How does this affect the brightness of the lightbulb?

● Cut a 2" (5 cm) square of heavy cardboard. Punch a hole in two opposite ends and insert a brass fastener or thumbtack into each hole. Attach a paper clip around one fastener. It should touch the other fastener when swung around. Attach this switch to the lightbulb. When the paper clip touches the other fastener, the bulb should light.

Notes & Observations

ELECTRIC LIGHTBULB

Real-World Science and Technology ©1997 Creative Teaching Press

ELECTROMAGNETIC CRANE

66 An electromagnetic crane is simply a conventional overhead electric crane in which the up-and-down motion (the hook) carries an extremely large electromagnet. Its magnetic field is created by electricity, and therefore, can be turned on and off by the operator. Because this is a non-permanent magnet, the operator has the ability to attach and release loads. In order to pick up a load, a crane's magnet must be as heavy as the load. So, if you want to pick up a one-ton load, your magnet must weigh approximately one ton. To accommodate both the weight of the magnet and the load, the crane's capacity must be two tons. Interestingly, as magnetic metals get hotter, their magnetic efficiency is reduced. Eventually, a metal can get so hot that even an electromagnetic crane is almost unable to lift it. Magnetic cranes are used for loading scrap metals into furnaces for meltdown to make new metal, to load compacted automobiles onto railroad trucks, and to pick up delicate loads that can't be lifted by other methods. 99

**D. Larry Dunville, President,
Dearborn Crane & Engineering Co.,
Mishawaka, IN**

WHAT YOU NEED

scissors
small milk carton
3" x 6" (7.5 cm X 15 cm) cardboard
sharpened pencil
3–4' (1–1.5 m) insulated wire
wire cutters
nail
2 brass fasteners
D-cell battery
large paper clip
magnetic and non-magnetic
    objects (tacks, coins,
    nuts, bolts, poker chips)

CAUTION: Do not touch bare wire in a complete circuit. Use care when using scissors to poke holes.

1 Cut the top off the milk carton. Cut two 2" (5 cm) squares from opposite sides of the top edge of the remaining carton. Poke centered holes with a scissor point 1 ½" (4 cm) from the top of the other two sides.

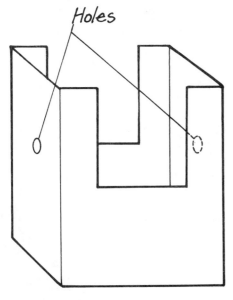

Holes

2 Fold up an inch (2.5 cm) on either side of the 3" x 6" (7.5 cm x 15 cm) cardboard.

3 With a pencil, poke aligning holes in the folded sides of one end of the cardboard.

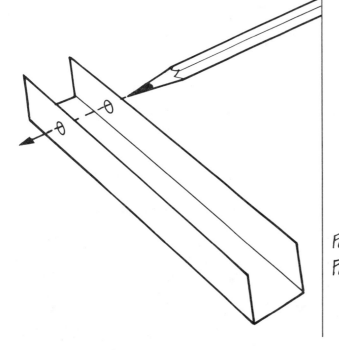

4 Coil insulated wire with stripped ends around a nail. Make each turn tight and even, just touching the one before. Leave at least 6" (15 cm) of wire off each end of the coil.

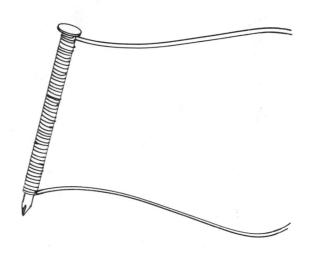

5 Push a brass fastener through the paper clip and the side of the milk carton. Push the other fastener through the carton about an inch (2.5 cm) away.

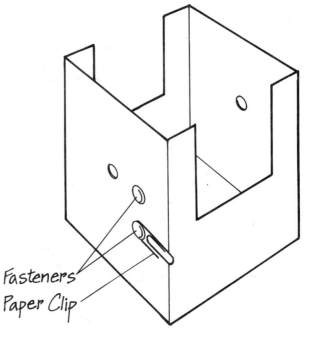

Fasteners

Paper Clip

Real-World Science and Technology ©1997 Creative Teaching Press

6 Attach one end of the wire from the nail to the brass fastener holding the paper clip and the other end of the wire to a battery terminal.

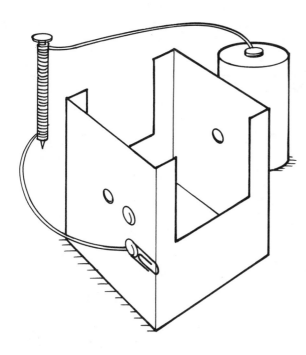

7 Connect another wire with stripped ends from the other fastener to the other battery terminal. Set the battery inside the milk carton.

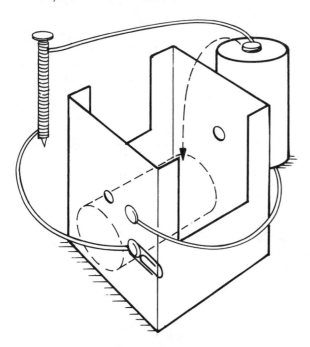

8 Run the pencil through a hole in the carton, the holes in the cardboard, and out the other hole in the carton.

9 Thread the nail and wire through the cardboard so the nail dangles off the end of the cardboard "jib."

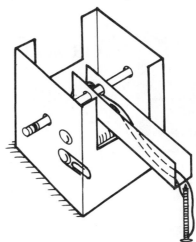

10 Touch the paper clip to the second brass fastener and hold the nail over a pile of magnetic and non-magnetic objects.

11 Raise the cardboard so the nail lifts magnetic objects out of the pile. Turn the "crane" and release the objects by moving the paper clip away from the fastener.

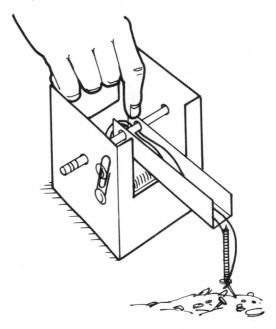

In a real electromagnetic crane, an electromagnet suspended from a long jib (the cardboard in this activity) attracts large pieces of scrap such as car and truck parts, motorcycles, rails, and other pieces of scrap metal. In this activity, touching the paper clip to the brass fastener completes an electric circuit, turning the nail into an electromagnet. When the paper clip is moved away, the current is switched off, and the nail loses its magnetism.

● Test the strength of your crane. How much can it lift at one time? Redesign the crane to increase its lifting power.

● Electromagnetism is also used to filter fine magnetic particles from the air in homes and offices. How might this be done?

● How might you use the crane to determine whether or not iron filings are present in sand? Could you filter other fine particles out of sand? How?

Notes & Observations

ELECTROMAGNETIC CRANE

Real-World Science and Technology ©1997 Creative Teaching Press

FUEL CELL

66 A fuel cell is nothing more than a very efficient battery. The difference between a conventional lead-acid battery (as found in a car) or a nickel-cadmium battery (as found in a flashlight) and a fuel cell is that a fuel cell has an external source of fuel constantly being pumped into it. This means that fuel cells do not drain as other batteries do. Fuel cells are very efficient—they produce little wasted heat energy. Most of the energy produced is usable electricity. Fuel cells are most commonly used in space travel or other areas where reliable energy sources, confined spaces, and waste by-products are concerns. One of the greatest advantages to using fuel cells in space travel is that the by-product of the energy produced is water. In space travel, water is in short supply and heavy to carry. Instead of carrying water as extra cargo, the crew uses water created by the fuel cells that power the spacecraft. 99

Michael J. West, Chemist

WHAT YOU NEED

newspaper
scissors
paper towels
hollow plastic hair roller
measuring spoons
graphite powder
3 small bowls
measuring cups
flour
water
string
1" x 4" (2.5 cm x 10 cm) galvanized
    steel strip
salt
alligator clips
galvanometer (pages 66–68)

WHAT YOU DO

CAUTION: Steel edges may be sharp—handle with care. Do not touch bare wire in a complete circuit.

1 Cover the work area with newspaper.

2 Cut a 12" (30 cm) paper towel strip slightly wider than the hair roller is long.

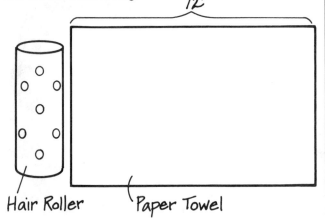

Hair Roller   Paper Towel

3 Place 2 teaspoons (10 mL) of graphite powder into a small bowl. In another bowl, mix $\frac{1}{8}$ cup (32 mL) flour and $\frac{1}{2}$ cup (125 mL) water. Slowly add this mixture to the graphite, stirring to create a thick paste.

4 Cover the entire width and about 4" (10 cm) of the length of the towel strip with the paste. Wrap the strip around the roller and secure it with string. Let the paste dry overnight.

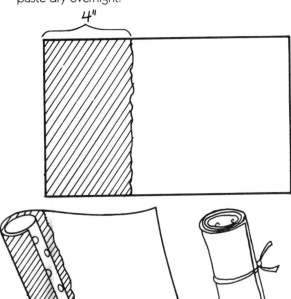

5 Insert the galvanized steel strip into the hair roller. It should fit snugly inside.

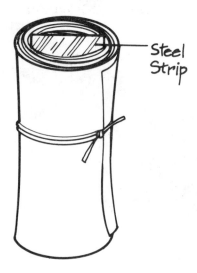

Steel Strip

6 Mix a heaping tablespoon (15 mL) of salt into a bowl of hot water and stir until dissolved. Stand the "fuel cell" in the salt water.

7 Using alligator clips, attach one wire from the galvanometer to the paste-covered towel and roller. Attach the other wire from the galvanometer to the steel strip.

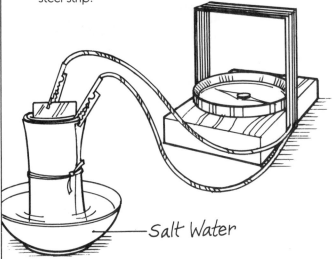

Salt Water

8 Observe the needle on the galvanometer. It should move, indicating that the fuel cell is generating electricity.

Real-World Science and Technology ©1997 Creative Teaching Press

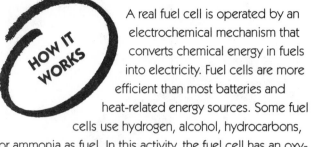

A real fuel cell is operated by an electrochemical mechanism that converts chemical energy in fuels into electricity. Fuel cells are more efficient than most batteries and heat-related energy sources. Some fuel cells use hydrogen, alcohol, hydrocarbons, or ammonia as fuel. In this activity, the fuel cell has an oxygen electrode (the graphite allows oxygen in the air to enter the cell) and a steel electrode. The salt water functions as an electrolyte to conduct current from one electrode to another.

● Design a machine that uses a fuel cell. What are the advantages and disadvantages of using a fuel cell rather than other energy sources?

● Research and list in your technology journal machines powered by fuel cells. What types of electrodes do these cells use?

● Design a factory that uses fuel cells as its energy source.

Notes & Observations

FUEL CELL

GALVANOMETER

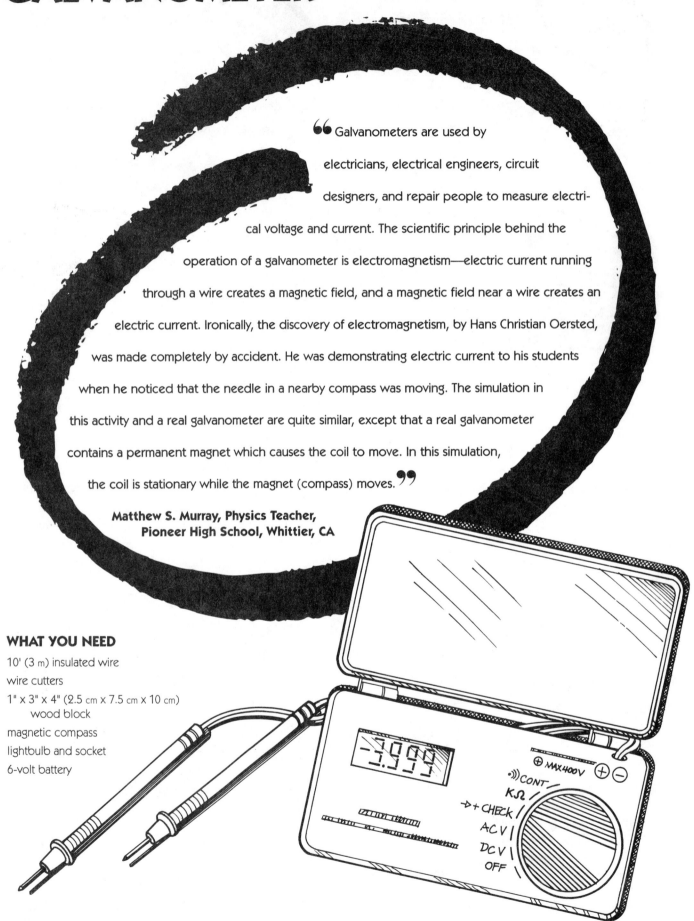

66 Galvanometers are used by electricians, electrical engineers, circuit designers, and repair people to measure electrical voltage and current. The scientific principle behind the operation of a galvanometer is electromagnetism—electric current running through a wire creates a magnetic field, and a magnetic field near a wire creates an electric current. Ironically, the discovery of electromagnetism, by Hans Christian Oersted, was made completely by accident. He was demonstrating electric current to his students when he noticed that the needle in a nearby compass was moving. The simulation in this activity and a real galvanometer are quite similar, except that a real galvanometer contains a permanent magnet which causes the coil to move. In this simulation, the coil is stationary while the magnet (compass) moves. **99**

**Matthew S. Murray, Physics Teacher,
Pioneer High School, Whittier, CA**

WHAT YOU NEED

10' (3 m) insulated wire
wire cutters
1" x 3" x 4" (2.5 cm x 7.5 cm x 10 cm)
    wood block
magnetic compass
lightbulb and socket
6-volt battery

CAUTION: Do not touch bare wire in a complete circuit.

1 Wrap wire with stripped ends around the wood block to create a large, rectangular coil. Leave about 2' (60 cm) of free wire at each end of the coil. Remove the coil from the block.

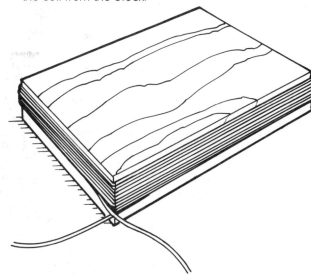

2 Set the compass on the block so the needle points north. Place the block and compass into the coil so the coil stands 1–2" (2.5–5 cm) over the compass.

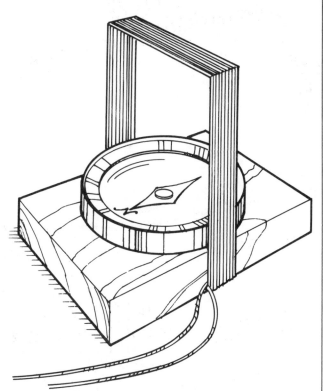

3 Attach one end of the wire coil to a lightbulb socket and the other to a battery terminal.

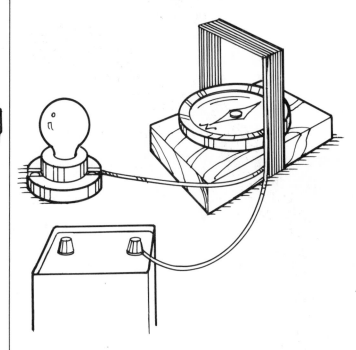

4 Using insulated wire, connect the lightbulb socket to the other battery terminal. Observe the compass needle, and record results in your technology journal.

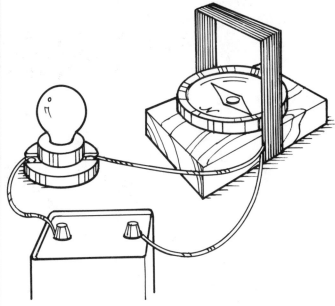

5 Reconnect the circuit to opposite battery terminals. Observe changes in the compass needle's movement, and record your observations.

HOW IT WORKS

A compass needle will point to Earth's magnetic north unless it is disrupted by a nearby magnetic field. Therefore, movement of the needle in this galvanometer indicates a nearby magnetic field. The principle of electromagnetism states that a current running through a wire creates a magnetic field. The compass needle's movement acts as a real galvanometer—indicating electric current.

STRETCHING TECHNOLOGY

● Design a scale for measuring the strength of an electric current. Attach the scale to the compass of your galvanometer and record the strengths of different batteries.

● Research Michael Faraday's first experiment with a galvanometer. Describe the experiment and its findings in your technology journal.

● Replace the lightbulb and socket with a wire coil. Observe the compass as you slide a bar magnet inside the coil. Electric current is created by electromagnetic induction. Research electromagnetic induction, and define and describe it in your technology journal.

Notes & Observations

GALVANOMETER

LOGIC CIRCUITS

66 Logic circuits are mechanical systems in which many complex series of tasks can be completed using specific commands. Not only are logic circuits driven by the initial input, but resulting output also functions as commands or instructions for the system's next task. One way to understand logic circuits is to think of an automatic sprinkler system. Water goes through certain pipes to water a portion of a lawn. When a preset amount of water has flowed through those pipes, valves redirect the water to another set of pipes to water a new portion of the lawn. Not only is the water what the system controls—it controls the system. The same thing happens in an electric logic circuit. An initial command begins the flow of electricity, and the course of that electricity causes a predetermined series of events to occur. Naturally, more complex machines will have more complex logic circuits. From computers to alarm clocks, logic circuits are a key component of all electronic devices. This activity effectively simulates a simple logic circuit because it illustrates how commands are specified to achieve desired results. 99

**Wes Lombardi, Electrical Engineer,
Delmage Digital**

WHAT YOU NEED

two 8 ½" x 11" (21 cm x 27.5 cm)
    cardboard pieces
pencil
6 brass fasteners
ruler
wire cutters
nine 15" (37.5 cm) insulated wires
3 lightbulbs and sockets
4.5-volt battery
glue
three 1" x 1 ½" (2.5 cm x 4 cm) foil strips
three 2" x 12" (5 cm x 30 cm) cardboard strips
stapler

WHAT YOU DO

CAUTION: Do not touch bare wire in a complete circuit.

1 On both large cardboard pieces, mark lines dividing the width into three equal sections.

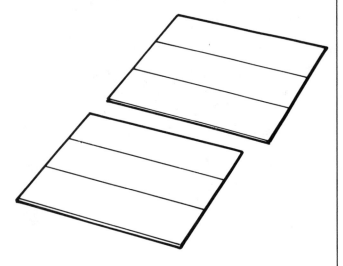

2 On one piece, insert two brass fasteners 3" (7.5 cm) from the end of the first section, 6" (15 cm) from the end of the next section, and 9" (22.5 cm) from the end of the last.

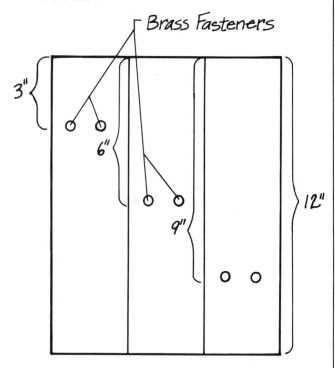

Brass Fasteners

3"
6"
9"
12"

3 With wire cutters, strip the insulation off the ends of the wires.

4 Place three lightbulbs in sockets at one end of the cardboard.

5 Connect wires from the lightbulbs to the negative terminal of the battery. Use the other wires to connect the left fastener in each pair to a lightbulb and the right fastener to the positive terminal of the battery.

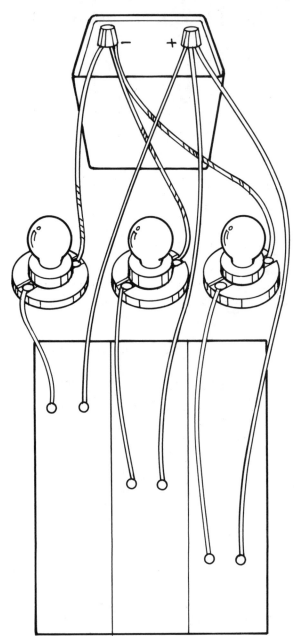

− +

6 Glue the foil strips to the narrow cardboard strips at the same positions as the fasteners on the large cardboard. Touch the foil strips to pairs of fasteners to see if a circuit is completed (to test the connections).

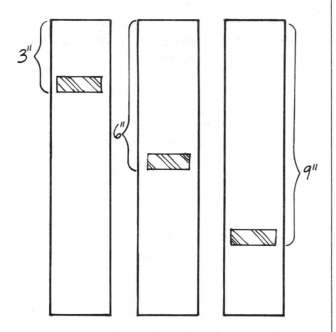

7 Staple the other large piece of cardboard on top of the first piece along the lines that divide it into thirds.

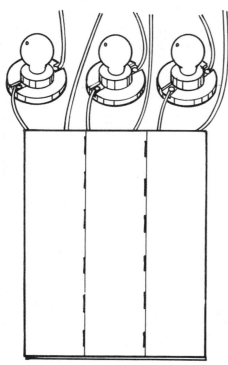

8 Randomly choose one of the narrow strips and push it into the first sleeve in the board. If the aluminum strip touches a pair of fasteners, the bulb will light because a connection is made.

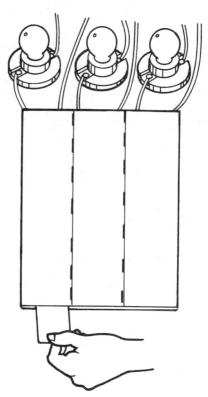

9 Make a chart in your technology journal that shows which cardboard strips light each bulb.

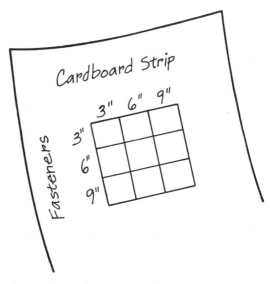

HOW IT WORKS

In a real computer circuit board, circuits are arranged so each command completes a specific series of circuits to perform a given function. For example, a command telling a computer to open a program completes a different set of circuits than a command telling it to close the program. In this simulation, the narrow strips represent commands. Each one completes a specific circuit, activating a desired function. In this case, the connection of a foil strip to a brass fastener completes a circuit which lights a bulb. If no connection is made, the circuit is incomplete and there is no pathway for the electricity to follow to the bulb.

STRETCHING TECHNOLOGY

● Design other logic circuits using wire, batteries, lightbulbs, and cardboard.

● Replace the lightbulbs with other electronic devices to make your logic circuits carry out various functions.

● With permission, disassemble an old computer to examine its circuit boards.

● Interview an electrical engineer and record your interview in your technology journal. Prepare questions beforehand and share results with classmates.

LOGIC CIRCUITS

Notes & Observations

Real-World Science and Technology ©1997 Creative Teaching Press

MAGNETIC LEVITATION TRAIN

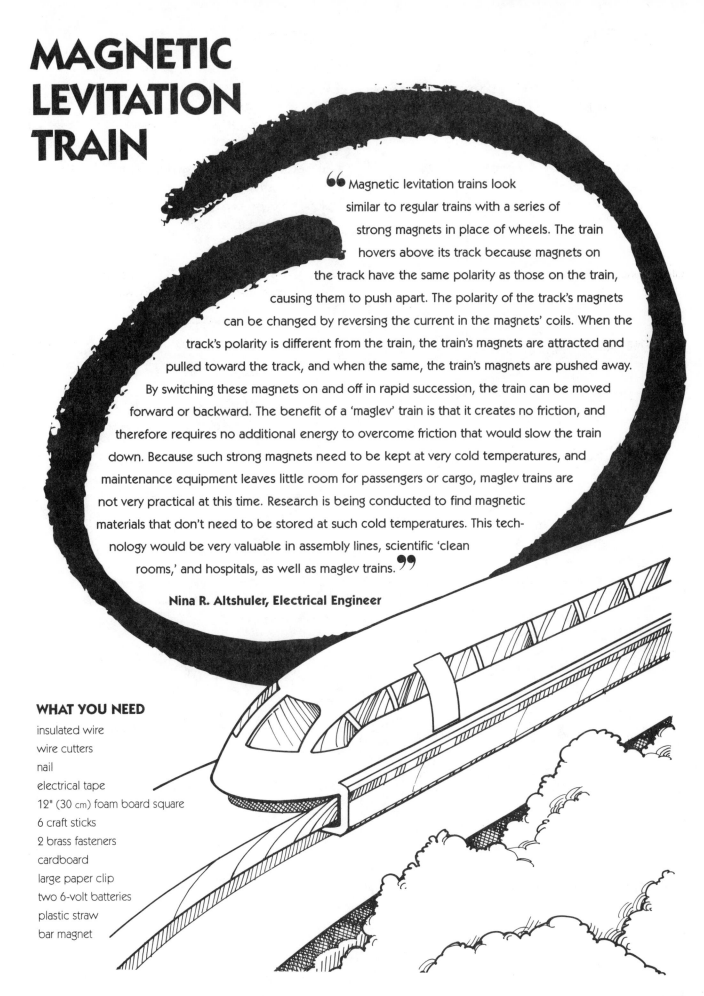

66 Magnetic levitation trains look similar to regular trains with a series of strong magnets in place of wheels. The train hovers above its track because magnets on the track have the same polarity as those on the train, causing them to push apart. The polarity of the track's magnets can be changed by reversing the current in the magnets' coils. When the track's polarity is different from the train, the train's magnets are attracted and pulled toward the track, and when the same, the train's magnets are pushed away. By switching these magnets on and off in rapid succession, the train can be moved forward or backward. The benefit of a 'maglev' train is that it creates no friction, and therefore requires no additional energy to overcome friction that would slow the train down. Because such strong magnets need to be kept at very cold temperatures, and maintenance equipment leaves little room for passengers or cargo, maglev trains are not very practical at this time. Research is being conducted to find magnetic materials that don't need to be stored at such cold temperatures. This technology would be very valuable in assembly lines, scientific 'clean rooms,' and hospitals, as well as maglev trains. 99

Nina R. Altshuler, Electrical Engineer

WHAT YOU NEED

insulated wire
wire cutters
nail
electrical tape
12" (30 cm) foam board square
6 craft sticks
2 brass fasteners
cardboard
large paper clip
two 6-volt batteries
plastic straw
bar magnet

73

CAUTION: Do not touch bare wire in a complete circuit.

1 Make an electromagnet by wrapping wire with stripped ends around the nail 50–60 times. Tape it to the middle of the foam board.

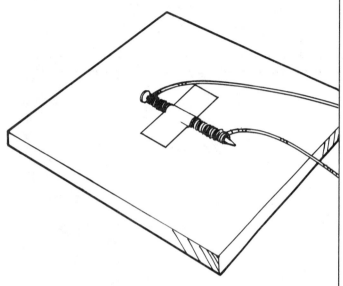

2 Push craft sticks into the foam board to form a row of three evenly-spaced sticks on either side of the nail.

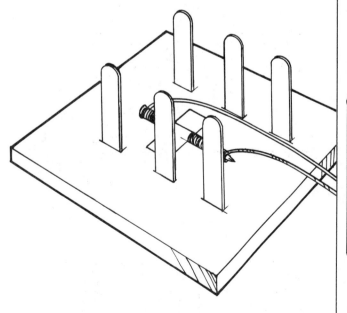

3 To make a switch, punch two brass fasteners an inch (2.5 cm) apart through a small piece of cardboard. Hook the paper clip onto one fastener. (Be sure it can touch the other fastener.)

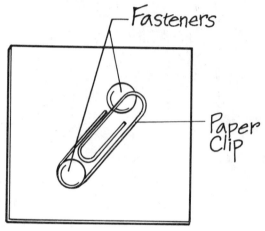

Fasteners

Paper Clip

4 Connect a short wire with stripped ends from the positive terminal on one battery to the negative terminal on the other.

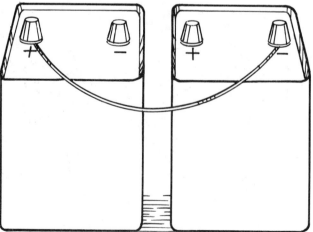

Real-World Science and Technology ©1997 Creative Teaching Press

5 Connect a wire from one end of the nail to the free terminal of one battery.

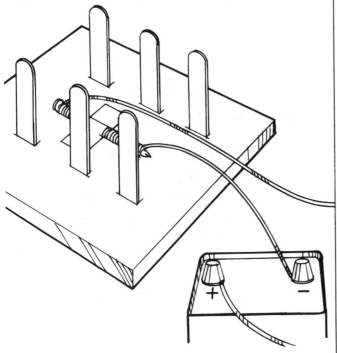

7 Tape the magnet to the middle of the plastic straw.

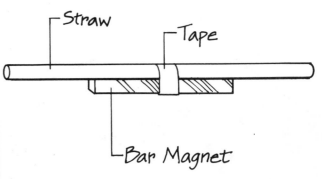

8 Hold the straw with the magnet over the nail and connect the switch. Let go of the straw. The electromagnet should repel the straw's magnet, making it levitate above the nail. The craft sticks serve as guide to keep the "train" in place. (If the magnet is attracted to the nail, reverse the battery connections.)

6 Connect a wire with stripped ends from the free end of the second battery to the brass fastener with the paper clip. Connect the free wire from the electromagnet to the free fastener.

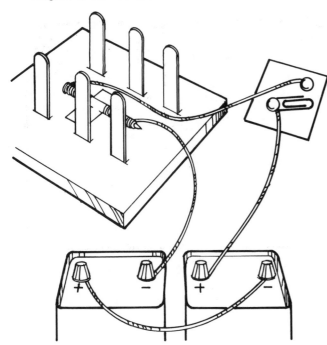

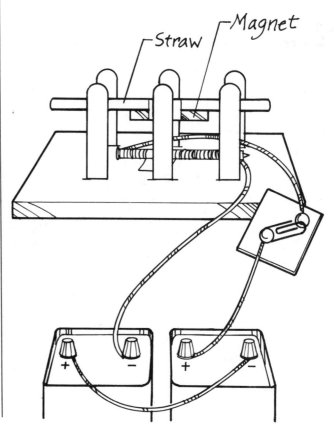

A real magnetic levitation train has no wheels. The force of strong magnets push away from each other when electricity flows through them. The magnets are arranged so the like poles of the track magnets face the like poles of the train magnets. When turned on, the poles repel each other and lift the train clear of the track so it hovers above the rails—just like the magnet taped to the straw when you ran electricity through the nail. Since like poles repel, the straw floats above the electromagnet when the switch is "on." In an actual train, a series of switches similar to the one in this activity rapidly turn on and off to make the train move forward and backward.

● Increase and decrease the strength of the electromagnetic nail. What effect does this have on the bar magnet?

● List in your technology journal ways magnetic levitation trains are beneficial to the environment.

● Suggest and design other practical applications of magnetic levitation.

Notes & Observations

MAGNETIC LEVITATION TRAIN

Real-World Science and Technology ©1997 Creative Teaching Press

MICROPHONE

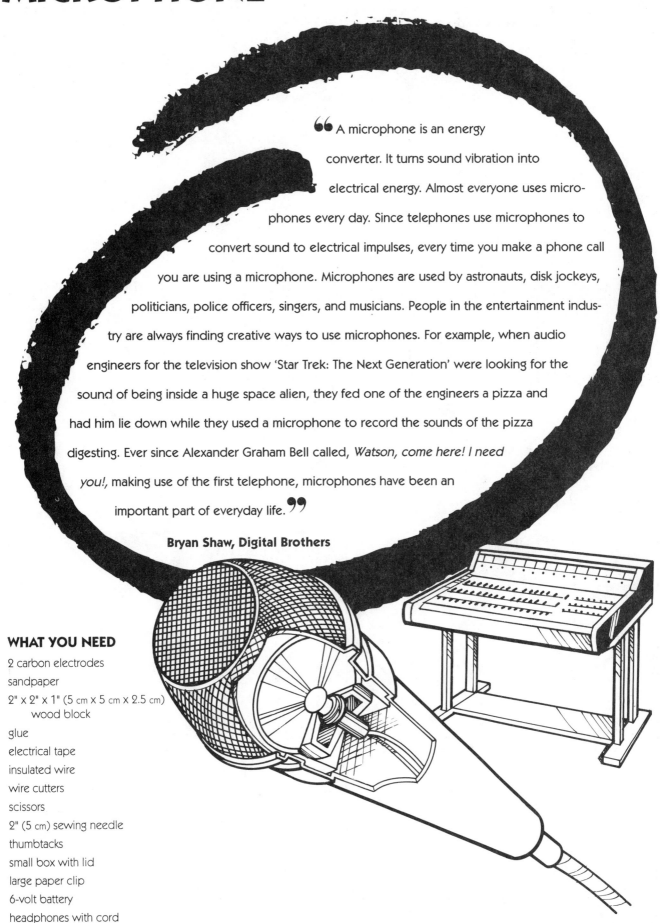

66 A microphone is an energy converter. It turns sound vibration into electrical energy. Almost everyone uses microphones every day. Since telephones use microphones to convert sound to electrical impulses, every time you make a phone call you are using a microphone. Microphones are used by astronauts, disk jockeys, politicians, police officers, singers, and musicians. People in the entertainment industry are always finding creative ways to use microphones. For example, when audio engineers for the television show 'Star Trek: The Next Generation' were looking for the sound of being inside a huge space alien, they fed one of the engineers a pizza and had him lie down while they used a microphone to record the sounds of the pizza digesting. Ever since Alexander Graham Bell called, *Watson, come here! I need you!*, making use of the first telephone, microphones have been an important part of everyday life. 99

Bryan Shaw, Digital Brothers

WHAT YOU NEED

2 carbon electrodes
sandpaper
2" x 2" x 1" (5 cm x 5 cm x 2.5 cm)
    wood block
glue
electrical tape
insulated wire
wire cutters
scissors
2" (5 cm) sewing needle
thumbtacks
small box with lid
large paper clip
6-volt battery
headphones with cord

Real-World Science and Technology ©1997 Creative Teaching Press

CAUTION: Use care when handling the scissors and sewing needle.

1 Flatten one side of each electrode with sandpaper.

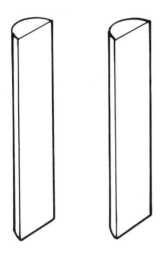

2 Glue the flat sides of the electrodes to opposite sides of the wood block. Part of the electrodes should extend off the block.

Electrodes

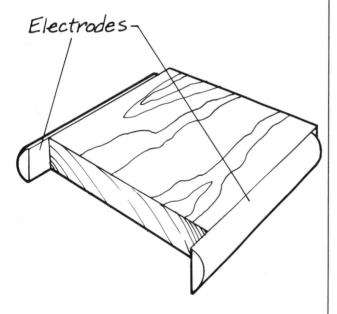

3 Tape a long insulated wire with stripped ends to each electrode near the point where the electrode meets the bottom of the wood block.

Wires

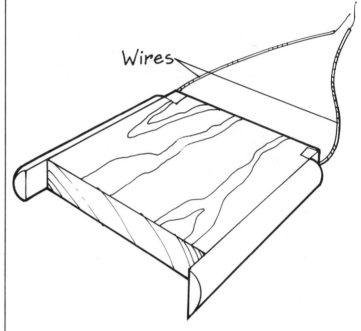

4 With a scissor point, carve a small notch in the flat side of each electrode ½" (1 cm) from the end. Fit the needle loosely into the notches. This apparatus is your microphone.

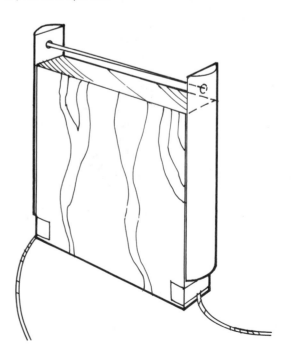

Real-World Science and Technology ©1997 Creative Teaching Press

5 Using thumbtacks, attach the wood block to the middle of the box lid.

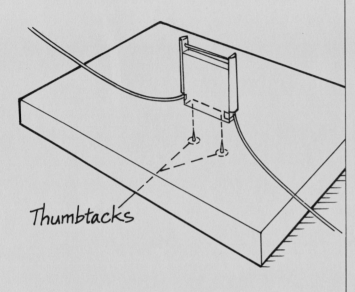

Thumbtacks

6 With a scissor point, poke four holes in the box lid—one on either side of the microphone, and one in each of the bottom corners of the box lid.

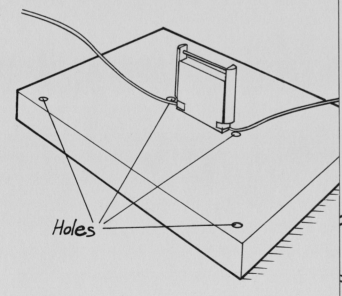

Holes

7 Run the wire from one electrode out the near hole, back through a hole in the corner of the lid, and attach it to a paper clip. Repeat for the other electrode's wire, running it through the unused holes and attaching it to a battery terminal.

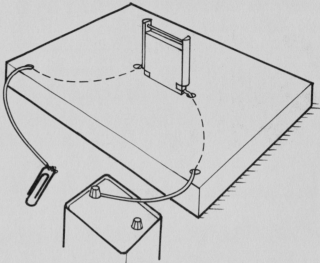

8 Securely tape the lid to the box, and stand the box on its side.

9 Remove the plug from the end of the headphone cord. Pull apart the two wires that make up the cord, and strip an inch (2.5 cm) of insulation off each. Attach one to the paper clip and the other to the free battery terminal.

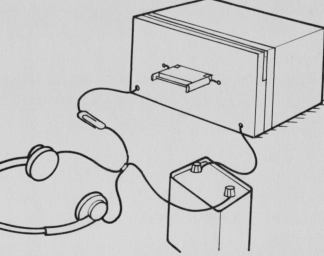

10 Put on the headphones and blow on the needle or tap the box with your fingers. You should hear amplified sound through the headphones.

HOW IT WORKS

Real microphones are highly sensitive to vibration. In your microphone, the needle vibrates when sound waves pass over it. These vibrations disturb the current flowing through the needle and electrodes. The disturbances cause vibrations in the headphones diaphragm identical to those created by the needle and electrodes. The headphones amplify the vibrations so they can be heard.

STRETCHING TECHNOLOGY

● Replace the needle with a pencil-lead rod or nail. Record sound quality differences in your technology journal.

● Change the position of the sound box. Lay it flat or place it against a wall. Record sound quality differences in your technology journal.

● Use different batteries and wires to experiment with the sensitivity of the microphone. Design a way to make your microphone as sensitive and clear as possible.

Notes & Observations

MICROPHONE

Real-World Science and Technology ©1997 Creative Teaching Press

PHOTOCOPIER

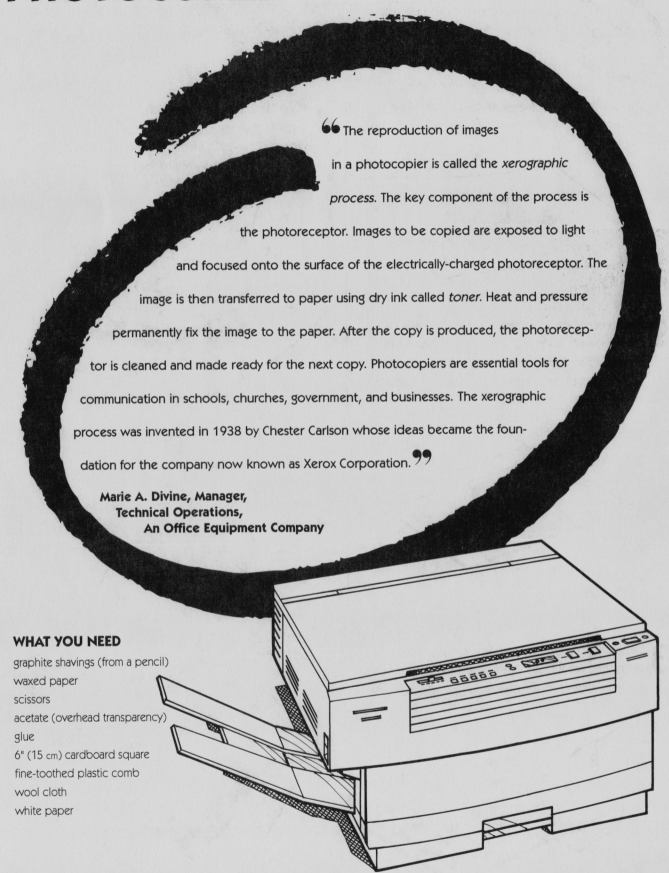

66 The reproduction of images in a photocopier is called the *xerographic process*. The key component of the process is the photoreceptor. Images to be copied are exposed to light and focused onto the surface of the electrically-charged photoreceptor. The image is then transferred to paper using dry ink called *toner*. Heat and pressure permanently fix the image to the paper. After the copy is produced, the photoreceptor is cleaned and made ready for the next copy. Photocopiers are essential tools for communication in schools, churches, government, and businesses. The xerographic process was invented in 1938 by Chester Carlson whose ideas became the foundation for the company now known as Xerox Corporation. 99

Marie A. Divine, Manager,
Technical Operations,
An Office Equipment Company

WHAT YOU NEED

graphite shavings (from a pencil)
waxed paper
scissors
acetate (overhead transparency)
glue
6" (15 cm) cardboard square
fine-toothed plastic comb
wool cloth
white paper

Real-World Science and Technology ©1997 Creative Teaching Press

1 Sprinkle a thin film of graphite shavings on waxed paper.

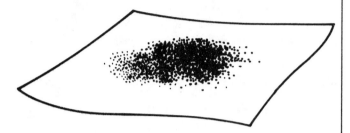

2 Cut several layers of acetate strips in the shape of a 5" (12.5 cm) letter, such as L or F, and glue them to the cardboard square so the letter appears backward. Glue several layers together so the letter is raised above the cardboard at least 1/4" (0.5 cm).

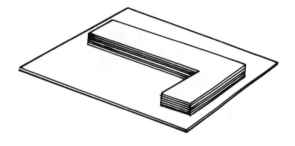

3 Electrically charge the plastic comb by rubbing it against the wool cloth. Carefully rub the comb against the letter to transfer the charge.

4 Hold the acetate letter an inch (2.5 cm) above the graphite shavings. The shavings should jump from the waxed paper to the letter. If they do not, repeat step 3 to be sure you transferred the electric charge.

5 Press white paper against your letter to create a permanent "copy."

White Paper

Acetate Letter

Real-World Science and Technology ©1997 Creative Teaching Press

HOW IT WORKS

In electrostatic photocopiers, a metal plate is charged with static electricity and exposed to the image to be copied. A light shines on the plate, leaving only the dark image charged. Toner blown across the plate sticks to the charged area, reproducing the image. The image is then transferred and fixed to paper. In this simulation, the graphite shavings represent the toner in a copier. Rubbing the charged comb against the letter is similar to transferring a static charge to the metal plate.

STRETCHING TECHNOLOGY

● Once the acetate loses its charge, the graphite shavings no longer stick to it. Create a way to make permanent reproductions of images.

● Research Chester Carlson's original xerographic process and compare it to the copying process in a modern photocopier. Record findings in your technology journal.

Notes & Observations

PHOTOCOPIER

PRINTED CIRCUIT BOARD

❝ A printed circuit board is the path by which an input source of electric power reaches its output destination. In this experiment, a battery is the source of power and a lightbulb is the destination. Circuit boards are composed of conductors and insulators. Conductors are substances through which electricity flows easily, while insulators are the opposite—electricity does not flow through them, and they are used to cover conductors for safety reasons. Circuit boards are used in any electrical device that is either plugged in or operated by batteries. From computer manufacturers to electricians to car designers, printed circuit boards are used in hundreds of occupations. The printed circuit boards in my line of work, computers, are all run by the binary system of numbers in which different combinations of 1s and 0s make all the commands. An amazing thing about modern computer circuitry is its size. Computer circuitry of the 1950s and 60s filled entire rooms—now, computers can process even more information using microchips the size of pennies! ❞

**Raj Advani, Software Engineer,
California State University, Fullerton**

WHAT YOU NEED

pencil
cardboard
adhesive shelf paper
aluminum foil
scissors
glue
wire cutters
insulated wire
electrical tape
4.5-volt battery
lightbulb and socket

84

CAUTION: Do not touch bare wire in a complete circuit. Leave circuits connected for only short periods of time—foil may become hot.

1 Draw a design on cardboard similar to that in the diagram.

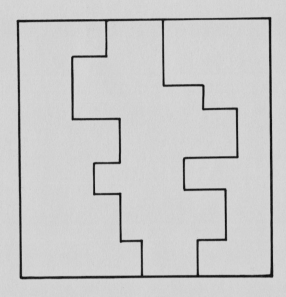

2 Attach adhesive shelf paper to a large square of aluminum foil, leaving about ¼" (0.5 cm) of foil exposed around the square. Cut several 1" (2.5 cm)-wide strips.

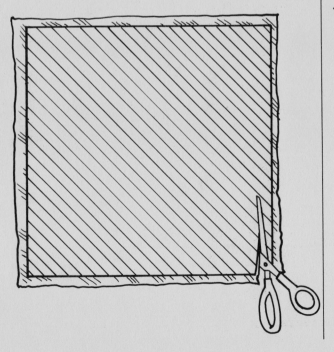

3 Glue the strips, foil side down, along the paths on the cardboard.

4 Strip the insulation off the ends of four 4" (10 cm) wires. Use the wires and tape to connect foil strips to the battery terminals at one end of the cardboard and foil strips at the other end to the lightbulb socket. The bulb should light.

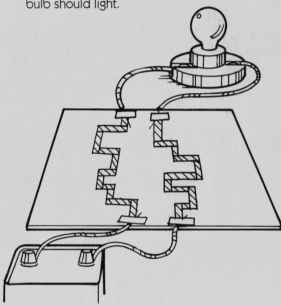

5 Cut a flap in a foil strip to make an on/off switch.

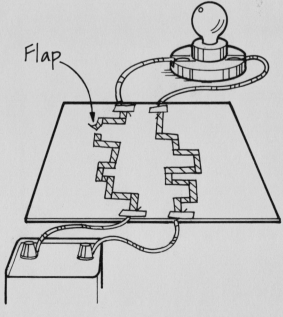

Flap

In your circuit board, the aluminum foil conducts electricity. When the wires touch the foil, they complete a circuit, lighting the bulb. The adhesive shelf paper acts as an insulator, a substance that does not conduct electricity. In a real circuit board, complex pathways are designed to conduct complex jobs. Because these pathways are stamped onto small silicon chips, machines can accommodate thousands of circuits in relatively small spaces.

● Use switches and extra foil strips to design more complex circuit-board pathways.

● Interview a computer technician, engineer, or programmer. Record your findings in your technology journal, and share what you learn with classmates.

● Research the manufacturing process of printed circuit boards and silicon microchips. Record your findings in your technology journal. Include information explaining why silicon is used to manufacture microchips.

Notes & Observations

PRINTED CIRCUIT BOARD

RADIO

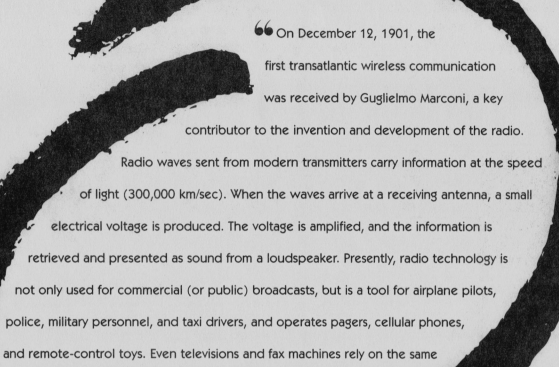

66 On December 12, 1901, the first transatlantic wireless communication was received by Guglielmo Marconi, a key contributor to the invention and development of the radio. Radio waves sent from modern transmitters carry information at the speed of light (300,000 km/sec). When the waves arrive at a receiving antenna, a small electrical voltage is produced. The voltage is amplified, and the information is retrieved and presented as sound from a loudspeaker. Presently, radio technology is not only used for commercial (or public) broadcasts, but is a tool for airplane pilots, police, military personnel, and taxi drivers, and operates pagers, cellular phones, and remote-control toys. Even televisions and fax machines rely on the same technology as radios! 99

**Pablo Garcia, Assistant Chief Engineer,
KUSC FM, 91.5 MHz, Los Angeles, CA**

WHAT YOU NEED

12" (30 cm) cardboard tube
pencil
ruler
12" (30 cm) foam board square
7 thumbtacks
10–15' (3–5 m) heavy bare copper wire
rubber bands
electrical tape
300 picofarad variable capacitor
silicon diode
earphone
wire cutters
insulated wire
large paper clip
long nail

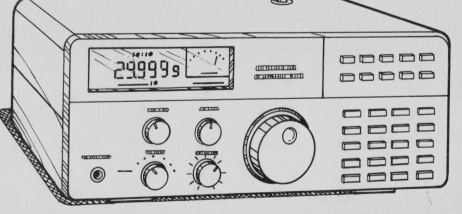

CAUTION: Handle capacitor and diode with care. Do not touch bare wire in a complete circuit.

1 Make pencil marks on the cardboard tube at 3 1/2" (9 cm), 4 1/2" (11 cm), 5 1/2" (14 cm), 7 1/2" (19 cm), and 9 1/2" (24 cm). Draw lines with the same spacing across the foam board. The marks on the tube should align with the lines on the board.

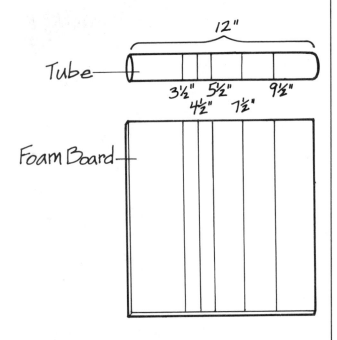

2 Insert a thumbtack halfway into each line in the middle of the board. These tacks mark your "stations."

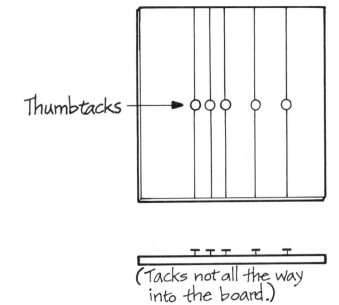

3 Tightly coil bare copper wire around the cardboard tube so each coil touches the next. When you reach each line on the tube, extend the wire away from the tube and wrap it around the thumbtack in the matching line. Leave 10–12" (25–30 cm) of wire extending from the end of the coil.

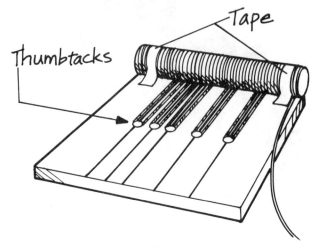

4 Secure the wire coil to the tube at each end with a rubber band. Tape the tube near the back edge of the foam board.

5 Align a tack with the wire extending from the end of the coil about 5" (12.5 cm) from the tube. Insert the tack halfway into the board.

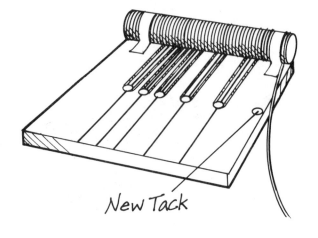

Real-World Science and Technology ©1997 Creative Teaching Press

6 Wrap the wire around the tack at a 90° angle, and connect the wire to an end of the capacitor.

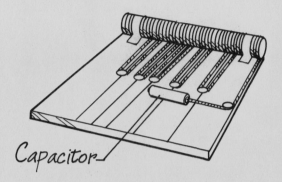

Capacitor

7 Align a tack with the other end of the tube and insert it halfway into the board. Attach a bare wire to the free end of the capacitor, wrap it around the tack, and connect it to the diode.

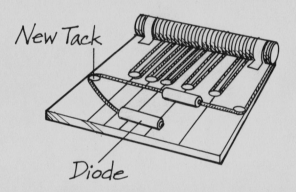

New Tack

Diode

8 Connect a wire from the free end of the diode to the earphone. Connect a wire from the earphone to the tack from step 5.

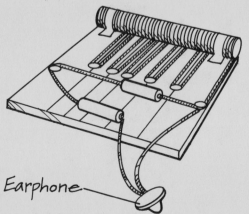

Earphone

9 Attach an insulated wire with stripped ends to the tack from step 7. Connect the paper clip to the other end. The wire should be long enough for the paper clip to touch each of the five station tacks.

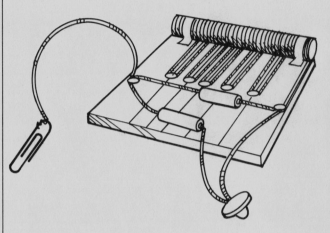

10 To make a ground connection, attach a long insulated wire with stripped ends to the tack from step 5. Connect the nail to the other end, and let it rest on the ground.

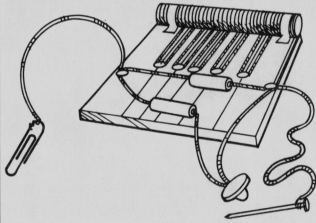

11 To make the antenna, extend a long insulated wire from the tack in step 7. If possible, attach it to a tall metal object.

12 Touch the paper clip to one of the station tacks and listen closely to the earphone. You might hear anything from from faint static to a fairly clear signal from a local radio station. Touch the paper clip to other station tacks and compare what you hear.

In a radio transmitter, sounds are converted into electrical signals. These signals, or waves, are received by an antenna (in this case, a long wire) attached to a radio. The radio's capacitor can receive signals at different frequencies. (Each radio station transmits signals at a different frequency.) These signals are converted back to the original sounds by speakers or earphones.

STRETCHING TECHNOLOGY

● Experiment with the number of coils and the length of the antenna. Try to make the radio's reception clearer and add more stations.

● Research ham radio operation. If your community has a ham radio club, invite a member to talk to your class about operating ham radios. Record your findings in your technology journal.

Notes & Observations

RADIO

SOLAR ELECTRIC CELL

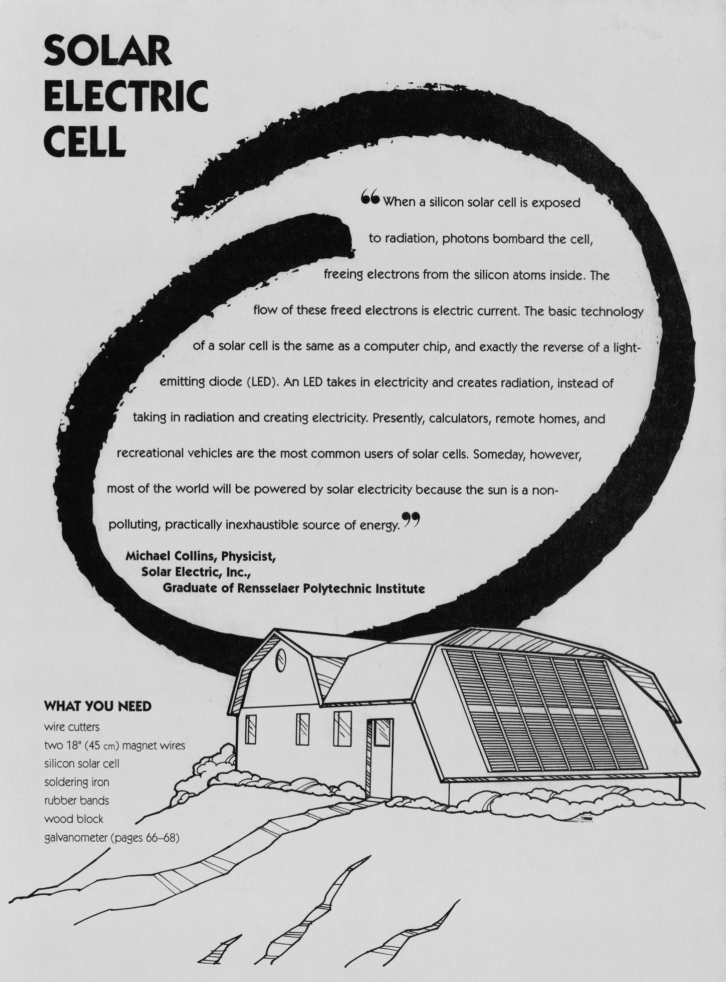

66 When a silicon solar cell is exposed to radiation, photons bombard the cell, freeing electrons from the silicon atoms inside. The flow of these freed electrons is electric current. The basic technology of a solar cell is the same as a computer chip, and exactly the reverse of a light-emitting diode (LED). An LED takes in electricity and creates radiation, instead of taking in radiation and creating electricity. Presently, calculators, remote homes, and recreational vehicles are the most common users of solar cells. Someday, however, most of the world will be powered by solar electricity because the sun is a non-polluting, practically inexhaustible source of energy. 99

**Michael Collins, Physicist,
Solar Electric, Inc.,
Graduate of Rensselaer Polytechnic Institute**

WHAT YOU NEED

wire cutters
two 18" (45 cm) magnet wires
silicon solar cell
soldering iron
rubber bands
wood block
galvanometer (pages 66–68)

CAUTION: Use the soldering iron carefully—touch only the handle when it is on. The silicon solar cell is fragile—handle it carefully.

1 Remove the insulation from the magnet wire ends.

2 Solder the end of one wire to the silver edge of the solar cell and the other end to the opposite edge.

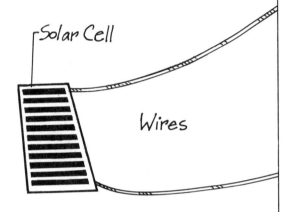

Solar Cell

Wires

3 Rubber-band the cell to the top of the wood block.

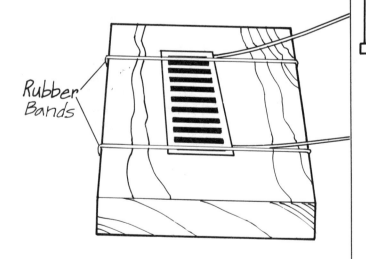

Rubber Bands

4 Connect wires from the solar cell to the galvanometer.

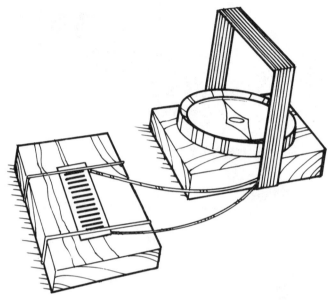

5 Place the cell in direct sunlight.

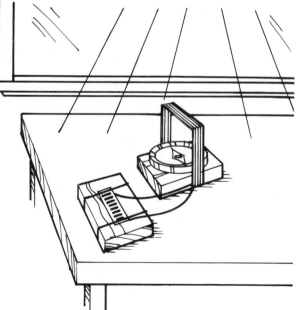

6 Observe the needle on the galvanometer, and record your observations in your technology journal.

Real-World Science and Technology ©1997 Creative Teaching Press

HOW IT WORKS

In a solar cell, sunlight is changed into electricity. When light strikes the cell, it frees electrons from the silicon atoms. The resulting flow of electrons travels through wires to provide electricity. In this activity, the needle on the galvanometer moves when an electric current is present in the solar cell.

STRETCHING TECHNOLOGY

● Redesign your house, school, or car to incorporate solar cells.

● Research different uses for solar cells and list them in your technology journal.

● Design a way to maximize the amount of sunlight collected by the solar cell. (Hint: A shoe box and aluminum foil are helpful materials.)

Notes & Observations

SOLAR ELECTRIC CELL

SPEEDOMETER

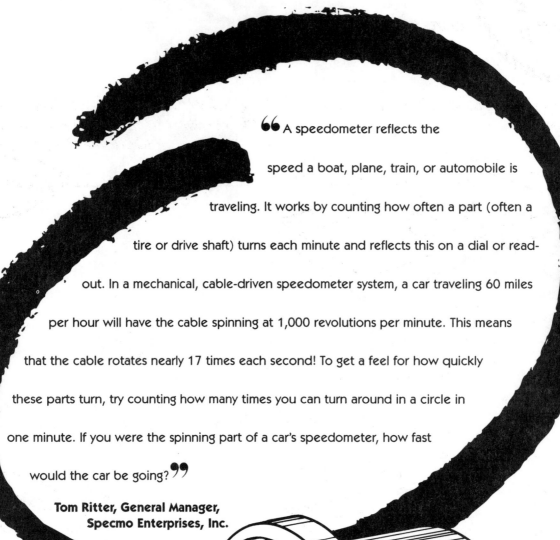

66 A speedometer reflects the speed a boat, plane, train, or automobile is traveling. It works by counting how often a part (often a tire or drive shaft) turns each minute and reflects this on a dial or read-out. In a mechanical, cable-driven speedometer system, a car traveling 60 miles per hour will have the cable spinning at 1,000 revolutions per minute. This means that the cable rotates nearly 17 times each second! To get a feel for how quickly these parts turn, try counting how many times you can turn around in a circle in one minute. If you were the spinning part of a car's speedometer, how fast would the car be going? **99**

**Tom Ritter, General Manager,
Specmo Enterprises, Inc.**

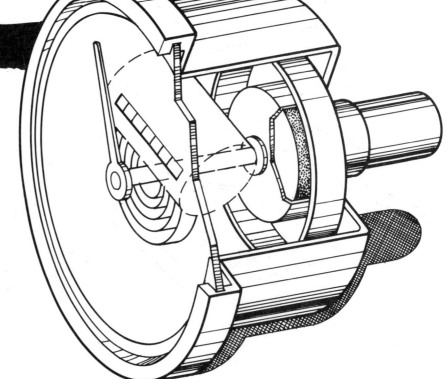

WHAT YOU NEED

modeling clay
shoe box lid
pencil with eraser
large sewing needle
cork stopper
aluminum pie pan
string
horseshoe magnet

CAUTION: Handle the needle with care.

1 Press a lump of modeling clay in the middle of the shoe box lid.

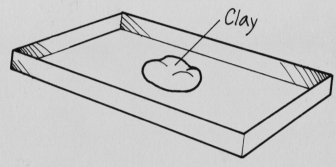

Clay

2 Use the pencil eraser to insert the sewing needle, eye first, into the cork stopper so the point sticks out of the top. Press the stopper into the modeling clay. Carefully separate the eraser from the needle.

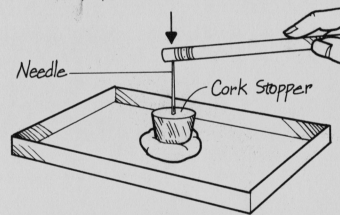

Needle

Cork Stopper

3 Invert the pie pan and balance it on the needle. It should be level and able to turn freely when spun.

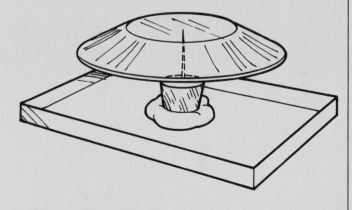

4 Tie a 12" (30 cm) string around the middle of the horse-shoe magnet. Tie the other end around the center of the pencil. The pencil acts as a handle for suspending the magnet.

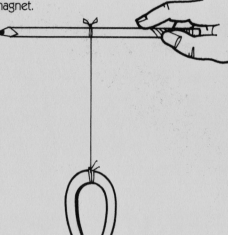

5 Dangle the magnet over the middle of the pan and twist it about 50 times. Let the magnet go. Observe the pie pan—it should spin in the same direction as the magnet.

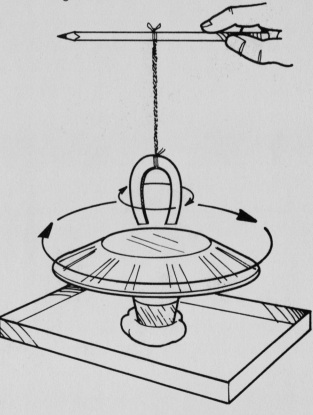

HOW IT WORKS

In a real speedometer, a magnet rotates at a speed proportional to the speed of the car. The spinning magnetic field around the magnet turns a piece of metal attached to a pointer on a scale that indicates the speed of the car (the speedometer). The metal in the speedometer moves in tandem with the magnet—either slowing down or speeding up as the rotating magnet changes speed.

STRETCHING TECHNOLOGY

● Design a speed scale to attach to your speedometer. Include a pointer to indicate the actual speed.

● Attach the magnet to a rotating motor. Vary the speed of the magnet's rotation and observe changes in the pie pan. How fast can you make the pan spin?

Notes & Observations

SPEEDOMETER

STEREO HEADPHONES

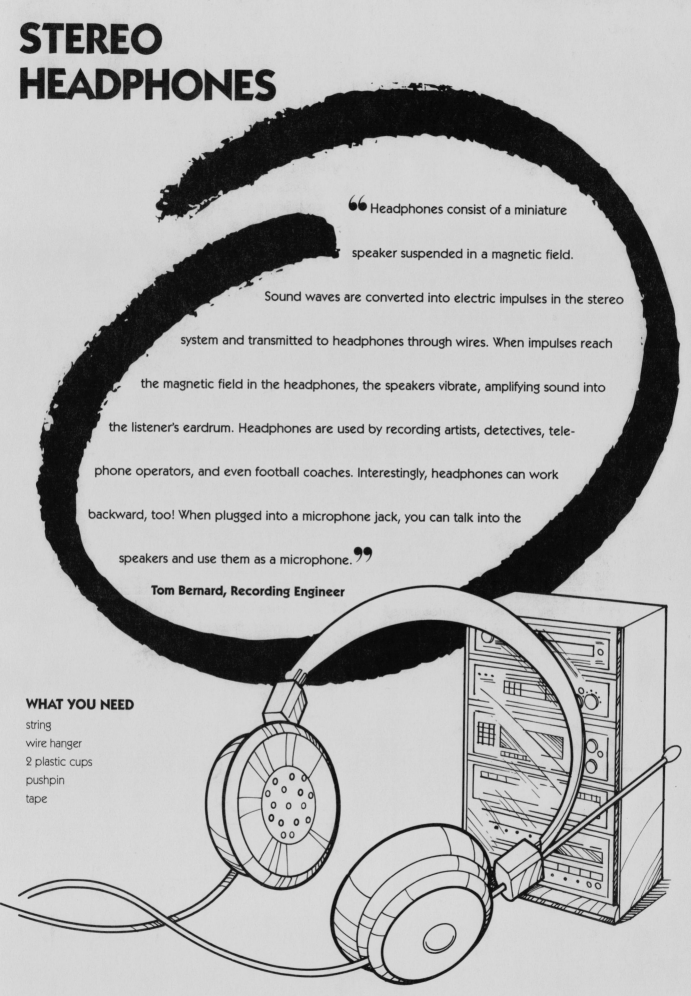

66 Headphones consist of a miniature speaker suspended in a magnetic field.

Sound waves are converted into electric impulses in the stereo system and transmitted to headphones through wires. When impulses reach the magnetic field in the headphones, the speakers vibrate, amplifying sound into the listener's eardrum. Headphones are used by recording artists, detectives, telephone operators, and even football coaches. Interestingly, headphones can work backward, too! When plugged into a microphone jack, you can talk into the speakers and use them as a microphone. 99

Tom Bernard, Recording Engineer

WHAT YOU NEED

string
wire hanger
2 plastic cups
pushpin
tape

1 Tie two 12" (30 cm) pieces of string to the bottom of the hanger. Leave about 6" (15 cm) between the strings.

6"

2 Poke a pinhole in the bottom of each plastic cup and thread a string from the hanger through each hole. Tie knots in the strings to fasten them inside the cups. (Tape the strings in place if the holes are too large.) The cups are your "headphones."

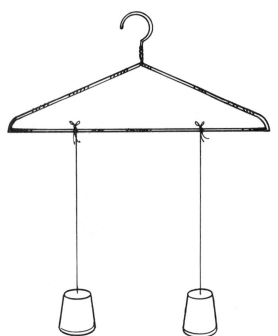

3 Put the cups over your ears and let the hanger drop so it taps against a hard surface such as a desk or table. Be sure the strings are pulled straight when the hanger drops. Do the headphones help you hear the hanger's vibrations?

4 Strike the hanger again, pinching off one string. Can you still hear sound in both ears? How are the strings like the wires attached to a set of headphones?

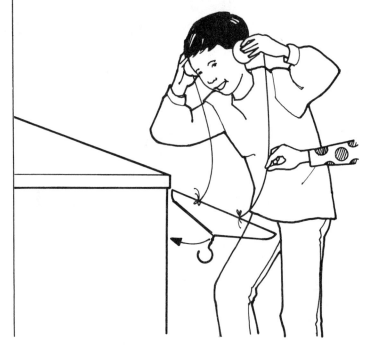

Real-World Science and Technology ©1997 Creative Teaching Press

HOW IT WORKS

Electronic headphones carry signals along thin wires and project sound through earpieces. These earpieces are usually padded around the outside for comfort and insulation from outside noise. The "headphones" in this activity carry vibrations, rather than electric signals, along strings to earpieces. The earpieces project the sound into your ears. Pinching one of the strings cuts off the vibration so the earpiece receives no sound to project. Disconnecting one of the wires from a set of real headphones would have the same effect.

STRETCHING TECHNOLOGY

● Design a way to improve your headphones. Try to make them project sound louder, and insulate them to prevent interference from outside noise.

● In your technology journal, draw and label a diagram showing how sound travels through your headphones. Include the metal hanger, strings, cups, air inside the cups, your ears, and the tabletop or desk.

● Attach one string from the headphones to a metal spoon. Tap the spoon against another spoon. How do the vibrations from the spoons sound different than the hanger? Do you hear the vibrations in "stereo" or "mono" sound?

Notes & Observations

STEREO HEADPHONES

TELEPHONE

66 By converting sounds to electric impulses and back again, telephones enable people to have conversations even though they are far apart. Telephones and similar devices, such as fax machines and computer modems, are used for voice communication, data transmission, and machinery operation. Most people use telephones in their homes every day, but some also rely on them as essential tools in their jobs. Salespeople, police dispatchers, engineers, stockbrokers, and office managers are some people whose jobs are made simpler by telephones. All the components in this simulation can also be found in a real telephone. Once you understand how this 'telephone' works, you should be able to understand a real one, too. 99

Anthony M. Signorelli, Product Applications Trainer, Samsung Telecommunications America

WHAT YOU NEED

metal can
can opener
aluminum foil
scissors
rubber band
wire cutters
insulated wire
cellophane tape
cardboard
graphite powder
6-volt battery
galvanometer (pages 66–68)

CAUTION: Do not touch bare wire in a complete circuit. Use care when handling the can—edges may be sharp.

1 Remove both ends of the metal can. Save one of the ends.

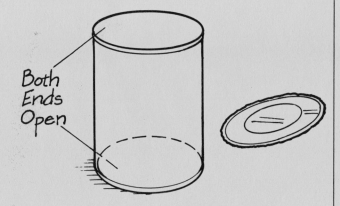

Both Ends Open

2 Cut a piece of aluminum foil larger than the opening of the can and secure it over one end with a rubber band.

Foil
Rubber Band

3 Tape the stripped end of an of insulated wire to the middle of the end of the can that was set aside.

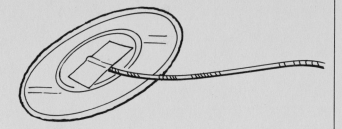

4 Wrap a strip of cardboard around the foil-covered end of the can and secure with tape. It should cover about half of the can and extend over the edge about 2" (5 cm).

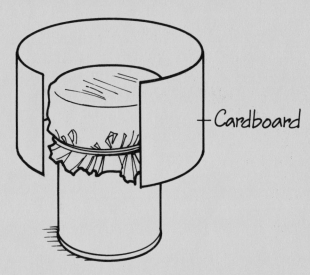

Cardboard

5 Fill the space on top of the foil inside the cardboard with graphite powder. Pack the powder loosely.

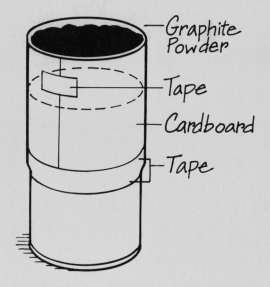

Graphite Powder

Tape

Cardboard

Tape

6 Place the can end on top of the graphite powder as a lid, and tape it down.

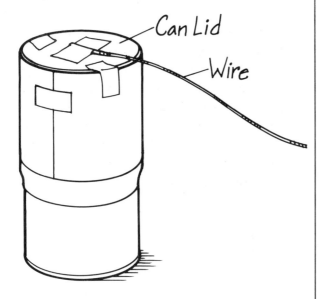

Can Lid

Wire

7 Connect the lid's wire to the galvanometer.

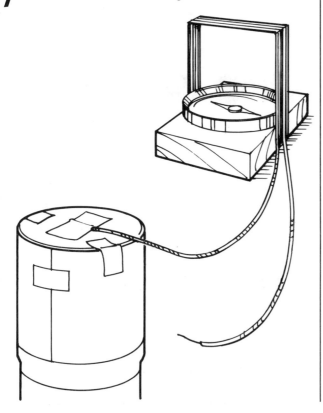

8 Use insulated wire with stripped ends to connect the battery to the galvanometer and the battery to the side of the can.

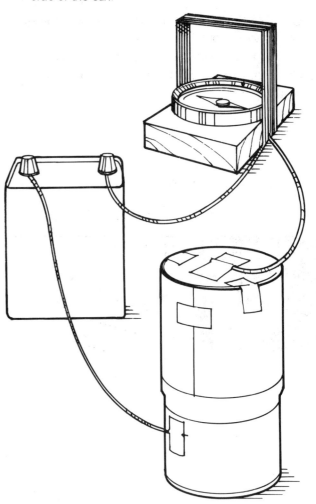

9 Speak into the open end of the can (opposite the foil diaphragm). Observe the galvanometer as the sound waves from your voice vibrate against the diaphragm.

HOW IT WORKS

In a real telephone mouthpiece, pressure waves caused by speaking act on a diaphragm in the telephone. The vibrations vary the current passing through carbon powder in the handpiece. The vibrations of the diaphragm induce weak electric impulses in a magnetic coil (like the galvanometer). The impulses travel down the end of the telephone line where they make similar vibrations in another diaphragm and are changed back to sound waves. These electrical variations correspond to the sound waves of your voice. In this activity, the graphite particles are electrically sensitive to movement. As a result, changes in pressure affect their conductivity.

STRETCHING TECHNOLOGY

● Vary the volume with which you speak into the "telephone." In your technology journal, record how the volume affects the movement of the galvanometer.

● Research Alexander Graham Bell's original telephone and Thomas Edison's improved version. Describe these inventions in your technology journal, and discuss them with classmates.

● Wrap a wire around a nail 10–15 times. (Keep the wire near the head of the nail.) Attach the wire ends to a battery. Fill a metal spoon with graphite powder, and level it off with the side of a pencil. Wrap the wires from the galvanometer around the spoon handle. Without touching the wire, hold the head of the nail over the graphite powder and note the movement of the galvanometer. This demonstrates what happens in a telephone's handpiece.

Notes & Observations

TELEPHONE

BAROMETER

66 Right now, air between your head and the fringes of the atmosphere is beating down on you at a pressure of about 1 kilogram per square centimeter. Fortunately, your body is designed to withstand this pressure, so you don't notice it. On Venus, however, the atmospheric pressure is about 90 times greater, so you would resemble a pancake if you lived there!

Barometers measure atmospheric (air) pressure. Every hour, airports and ships at sea measure air pressure and plot the readings on a map. Weather forecasters depend on these measurements to plot and track weather systems. Generally, low-pressure systems produce inclement weather, and high-pressure systems produce fair weather. Wind speeds can also be estimated by the barometric readings plotted on a weather map. If the lines on the map are close together, wind speeds are high; if the lines are far apart, wind speeds are low. As a marine weather forecaster, I collect a lot of statistics, but pressure readings from barometers are one of the most important for understanding and predicting weather. 99

**Charlie Fox, Lead Forecaster,
CFOX Pacific Weather Forecasting**

WHAT YOU NEED

large test tube
water
food coloring
2 glass tubes [2" (5 cm) long and
    6" (15 cm) long]
petroleum jelly
one-hole rubber stopper
6" (15 cm) narrow flexible tube
rubber bands
tape
ruler

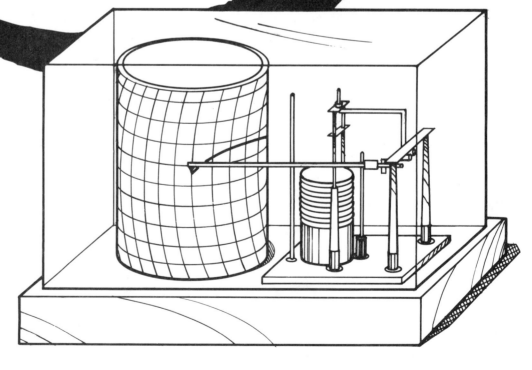

WHAT YOU DO

CAUTION: Glass tubes are fragile—handle with care.

1 Fill the test tube half full with colored water.

2 Lubricate the 2" (5 cm) glass tube with petroleum jelly, and insert it into the hole in the rubber stopper. Insert the stopper into the test tube.

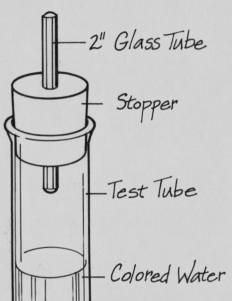

— 2" Glass Tube

— Stopper

— Test Tube

— Colored Water

3 Connect the glass tubes with the flexible tube.

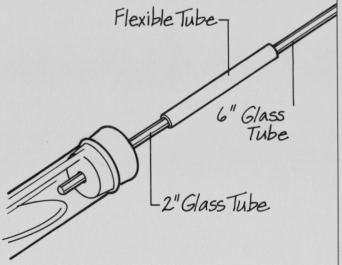

Flexible Tube —

6" Glass Tube

2" Glass Tube

4 Invert the test tube. Rubber-band the 6" (15 cm) glass tube to the test tube, and tape the entire assembly to the ruler.

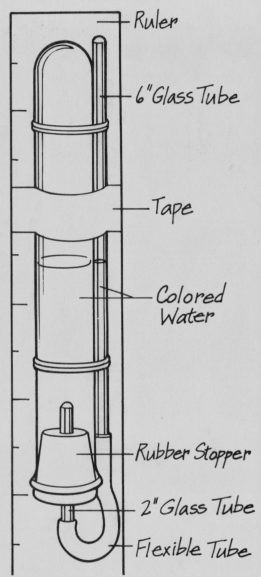

— Ruler

— 6" Glass Tube

— Tape

— Colored Water

— Rubber Stopper

— 2" Glass Tube

— Flexible Tube

5 Blow gently across the open end of the 6" (15 cm) tube until water from the test tube is forced into it. Using a ruler, measure and record the 6" (15 cm) tube's water level.

6 Keep daily records of changes in the tube's water level. This will reflect changes in air pressure.

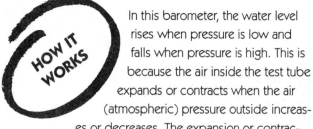

HOW IT WORKS

In this barometer, the water level rises when pressure is low and falls when pressure is high. This is because the air inside the test tube expands or contracts when the air (atmospheric) pressure outside increases or decreases. The expansion or contraction of air passing over the glass tube pulls air in or pushes it out. Changes in air pressure often precede weather changes. Meteorologists use barometers not only to measure air pressure, but also to predict weather patterns.

STRETCHING TECHNOLOGY

● Record daily barometer readings and weather observations in your technology journal. Describe any correlation between pressure changes and weather changes.

● Research how pressure changes affect weather and how meteorologists indicate air pressure on weather maps. Record findings in your technology journal.

● The temperature of the air affects barometer readings. Use a thermometer to find relationships between temperature and air pressure.

Notes & Observations

BAROMETER

Real-World Science and Technology ©1997 Creative Teaching Press

CAMERA

66 In many ways, the camera is similar to the eye. Light enters the eye through the lens, is adjusted by the pupil, and focused on the back of the eye. In a camera, light enters the lens, is adjusted by the aperture, and focused onto film. Both cameras and eyes invert images and have devices to convert images back to normal.

Cameras are used in a great number of careers, each specializing their camera for specific needs. For example, an advertising photographer uses different cameras than sports and underwater photographers. And photographers are not the only professionals that use cameras. Police investigator and surgeon are two other professions that depend on cameras in their workplace. Not too many people realize this, but photography is the most popular hobby in the world! If you've ever taken a picture, you're a photographer! 99

**Michael Jarrett, Advertising Photographer,
Michael Jarrett Studio**

WHAT YOU NEED

masking tape
shoe box with lid
cardboard tube
pencil
scissors
tracing paper
rubber bands
black construction paper
pushpin
modeling clay

WHAT YOU DO

CAUTION: Use care when cutting through thick materials.

1 Tape the lid onto the box. Be sure no light can enter the box.

2 Place the end of the cardboard tube against one end of the box and trace around it with a pencil. Cut out the circle.

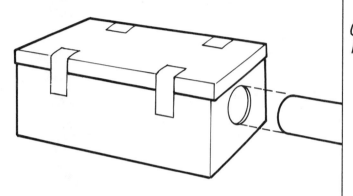

3 Cut a small hole at the other end of the box large enough to see through [about ¹⁄₂" (1 cm)-diameter].

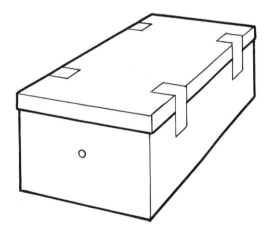

4 Cover one end of the tube with tracing paper, and rubber-band the paper in place.

5 Cover the other end of the tube with construction paper and secure it with rubber bands. Poke a pin-hole in the center of the paper.

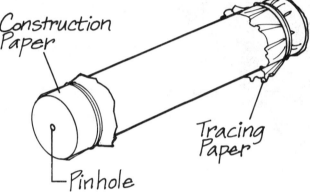

Construction Paper

Tracing Paper

Pinhole

6 Insert the tracing-paper end of the tube halfway into the box through the large hole. The construction-paper end should stick out like the lens in a real camera. Cover cracks between the tube and box with modeling clay so the only way for light to enter the box is through the pinhole.

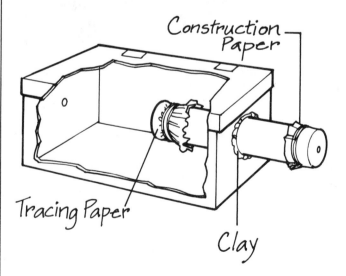

Construction Paper

Tracing Paper

Clay

7 Point the "camera" at a small, colorful object and look through the small hole in the back of the box. What do you see projected on the tracing paper?

Real-World Science and Technology ©1997 Creative Teaching Press

As light rays reflect off an object and pass through your camera's pinhole, they form an inverted image on the tracing paper. The pinhole in the cardboard acts like the lens of a camera, and the tracing paper collects the image just like film in a real camera. In a real camera, as well as in this simulation, the size of the image depends on the distance of the object from the pinhole and the distance of the pinhole from the tracing paper or film.

● Draw and label a diagram of your camera in your technology journal. Describe, in your own words, how a camera works.

● Research why lenses invert images and how cameras and eyes correct this inversion.

● Repeat the experiment with different-sized boxes and tubes, screens made of materials other than tracing paper, holes of different sizes, and different light sources. Can you make the image larger? smaller? clearer?

Notes & Observations

CAMERA

COLOR MONITOR

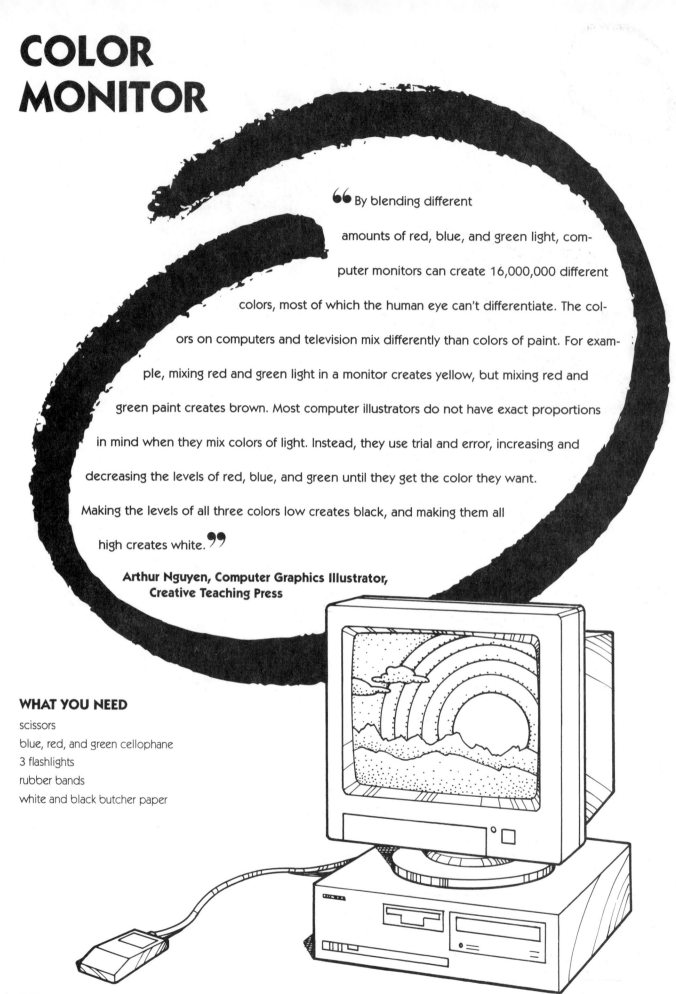

> **6 6** By blending different amounts of red, blue, and green light, computer monitors can create 16,000,000 different colors, most of which the human eye can't differentiate. The colors on computers and television mix differently than colors of paint. For example, mixing red and green light in a monitor creates yellow, but mixing red and green paint creates brown. Most computer illustrators do not have exact proportions in mind when they mix colors of light. Instead, they use trial and error, increasing and decreasing the levels of red, blue, and green until they get the color they want. Making the levels of all three colors low creates black, and making them all high creates white. **9 9**
>
> **Arthur Nguyen, Computer Graphics Illustrator,
> Creative Teaching Press**

WHAT YOU NEED

scissors
blue, red, and green cellophane
3 flashlights
rubber bands
white and black butcher paper

Real-World Science and Technology ©1997 Creative Teaching Press

WHAT YOU DO

1 Cut blue, red, and green cellophane to fit over the ends of the flashlights. Secure each piece with a rubber band.

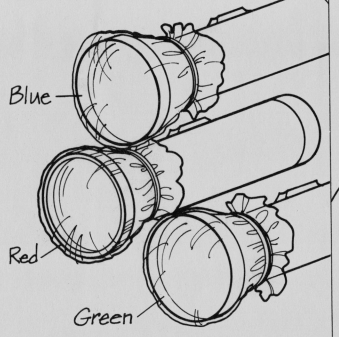

Blue —

Red —

Green

2 Cut out a large circle of white butcher paper and place it on a table.

Butcher Paper

3 Turn on the flashlights and turn out the lights.

4 Aim the flashlights at the paper. Slowly move the colored beams closer together so their edges touch; then closer so half the beams overlap, creating white light in the center.

White Paper — White Light

Colored Beams

5 Exchange the white paper for black. Repeat steps 3 and 4. How are the results different?

Colored cellophane filters white light into its component parts. When you look through the cellophane, only light of the same color reaches your eyes—the cellophane filters out all other colors. When you move the filters closer together, you mix the primary colors of light—red, blue, and green. (Note that these are different from the primary colors of paint—red, blue, and yellow.) Each colored light ray has its own wavelength. Mixing colors together combines different wavelengths. The screen on your computer or television combines colors by mixing tiny points of light. By mixing the three primary colors in different combinations, any color—including white and black—can be produced.

● A secondary color is an equal mixture of two primary colors. Experiment with blending two or three colors in different proportions. What colors can you create? Make a chart that lists these "additive" colors and their color components.

● Make a Newton's Color Disk by dividing a 10" (25 cm)-diameter cardboard disk into twelve equal sections of seven different colors in the following order: two yellow, one orange, one red, three pink, one turquoise, one black, and three green. Insert a pushpin through the center of the disk and into a pencil eraser. Spin the disk. What colors appear?

Notes & Observations

COLOR MONITOR

FIBER OPTICS

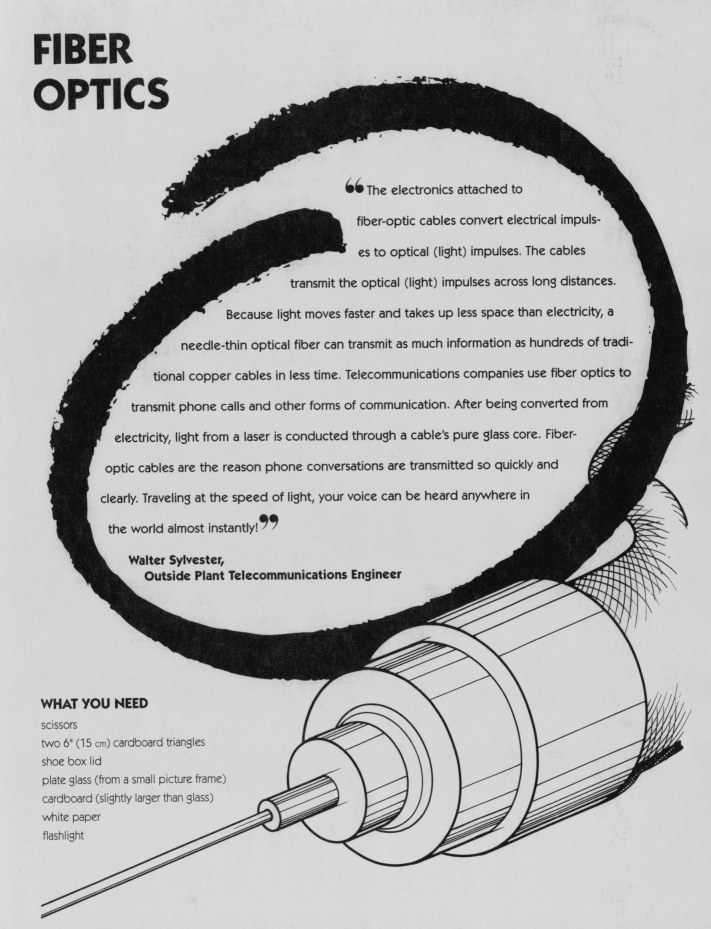

66 The electronics attached to fiber-optic cables convert electrical impulses to optical (light) impulses. The cables transmit the optical (light) impulses across long distances. Because light moves faster and takes up less space than electricity, a needle-thin optical fiber can transmit as much information as hundreds of traditional copper cables in less time. Telecommunications companies use fiber optics to transmit phone calls and other forms of communication. After being converted from electricity, light from a laser is conducted through a cable's pure glass core. Fiber-optic cables are the reason phone conversations are transmitted so quickly and clearly. Traveling at the speed of light, your voice can be heard anywhere in the world almost instantly! **99**

**Walter Sylvester,
Outside Plant Telecommunications Engineer**

WHAT YOU NEED

scissors
two 6" (15 cm) cardboard triangles
shoe box lid
plate glass (from a small picture frame)
cardboard (slightly larger than glass)
white paper
flashlight

CAUTION: Handle glass with care. Do not look directly into the light source.

1 Cut a slit from the top point to the middle of each cardboard triangle. Cut the bottom edge off the shoe box lid. Fit the lid into the triangles to make it stand.

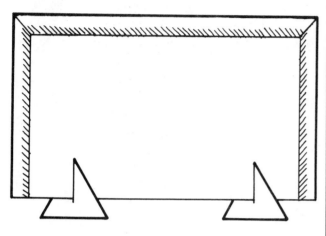

2 Lay the glass on the cardboard. Stand the shoe box lid at one end of the glass.

Glass   Cardboard

3 Slide a piece of white paper under the edge of the glass nearest the lid and curve it up so it rests against the shoe box lid.

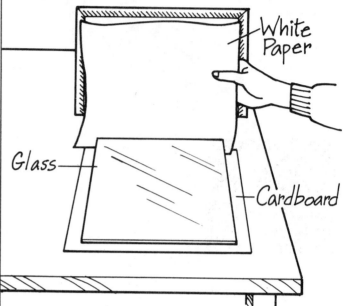

White Paper

Glass

Cardboard

4 Dim the lights. Lift the near ends of the glass and cardboard (opposite the box lid) slightly off the table, and shine the flashlight so the beam shines through the thickness of the glass. Colored light should appear on the paper.

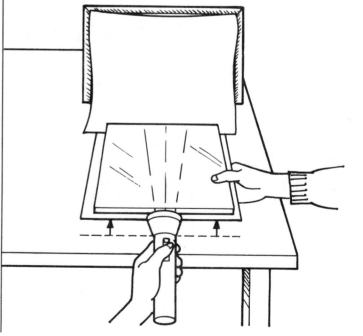

Real-World Science and Technology ©1997 Creative Teaching Press

In a real optical fiber, light rays generated by a laser travel through small glass fibers. These glass fibers are covered with materials that keep light reflecting within the fiber-optic cable. In this activity, light from the flashlight enters the edge of the glass and is reflected back and forth until it comes out the other edge and strikes the paper as a greenish-yellow glow. Because light from the flashlight is colorless, little or no light is visible within the glass, but impurities in the glass slightly break up the light as it passes through, creating the colored glow.

**STRETCHING
TECHNOLOGY**

● Research how telecommunications companies use fiber-optic cable. Find out where fiber-optic cable is used in your community.

● In this simulation, much light is lost out the sides of the glass. Design a way to minimize the amount of light lost so the light emerging from the glass will be as bright as possible.

● Fiber-optic cables can transmit pictures of a person talking on the phone as well as his or her voice. How might this technology, if widely implemented, affect a person's right to privacy? Discuss this controversial use of technology with classmates and in your technology journal.

Notes &
Observations

FIBER OPTICS

FIRE EXTINGUISHER

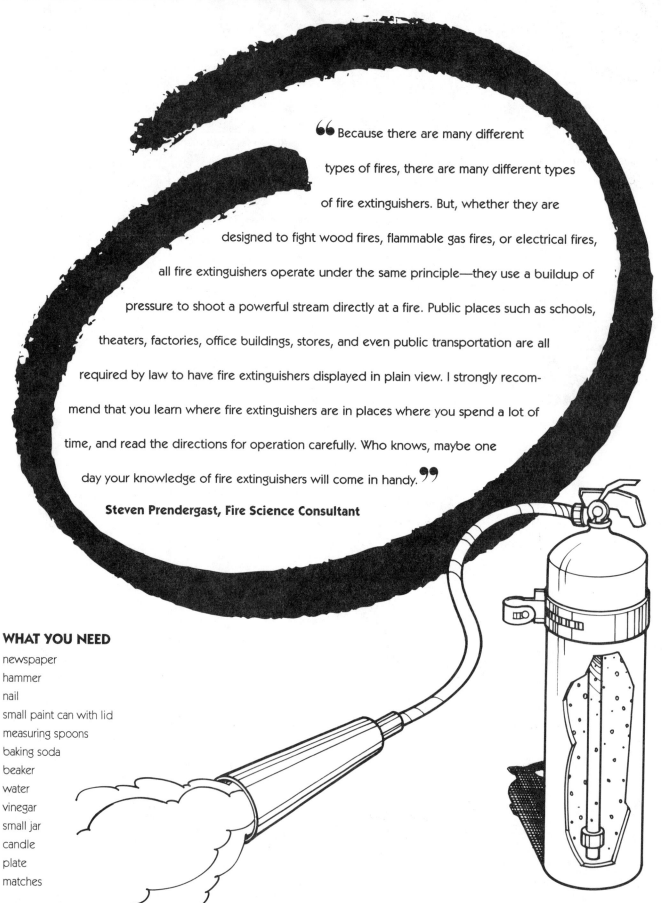

66 Because there are many different types of fires, there are many different types of fire extinguishers. But, whether they are designed to fight wood fires, flammable gas fires, or electrical fires, all fire extinguishers operate under the same principle—they use a buildup of pressure to shoot a powerful stream directly at a fire. Public places such as schools, theaters, factories, office buildings, stores, and even public transportation are all required by law to have fire extinguishers displayed in plain view. I strongly recommend that you learn where fire extinguishers are in places where you spend a lot of time, and read the directions for operation carefully. Who knows, maybe one day your knowledge of fire extinguishers will come in handy. 99

Steven Prendergast, Fire Science Consultant

WHAT YOU NEED

newspaper
hammer
nail
small paint can with lid
measuring spoons
baking soda
beaker
water
vinegar
small jar
candle
plate
matches

Real-World Science and Technology ©1997 Creative Teaching Press

WHAT YOU DO

CAUTION: Exercise extreme care when lighting and extinguishing flames and using the hammer and nail.

1 Cover the work area with newspaper.

2 Hammer a small hole in the center of the paint can lid.

Hole

3 Measure 2 tablespoons (30 mL) of baking soda into the beaker. Add water and stir until all the baking soda dissolves. Fill the paint can about one-third full with this solution.

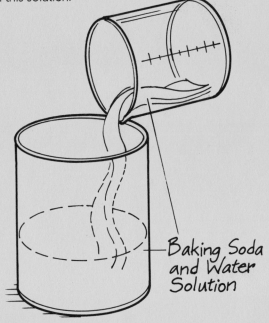

Baking Soda and Water Solution

4 Place 5 tablespoons (75 mL) of vinegar into the small jar and place the jar inside the can—make sure the baking-soda solution and vinegar do not mix.

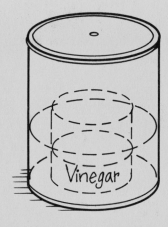

Vinegar

5 Place the lid securely on the paint can.

6 Place the candle on the plate and light the candle. Let some wax drip down the sides of the candle to fasten it to the plate.

7 Hold your finger over the opening in the can. Tilt it toward the candle, letting the vinegar and baking soda solution mix. Remove your finger from the hole. Extinguish the flame with the foam shooting out of the can.

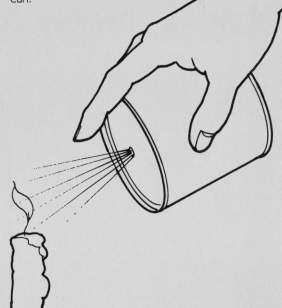

Real-World Science and Technology ©1997 Creative Teaching Press

HOW IT WORKS

The chemical reaction between the acetic acid in vinegar and the bicarbonate in baking soda creates a large volume of carbon dioxide gas. Blocking the hole in the paint can increases the pressure of the gas. Exposing the hole releases the pressure and forces the gas and chemicals out in a powerful jet of foam. The gas surrounds the candlewick and cuts off the oxygen-fueled fire. Deprived of oxygen, the fire is extinguished. A real fire extinguisher uses a similar pressure mechanism to shoot a foaming agent onto a burning object. By separating the object from the flame, it cuts off the oxygen and extinguishes the fire.

STRETCHING TECHNOLOGY

● From how far away can your fire extinguisher put out a fire? Redesign your model to maximize its force and duration.

● Fire extinguishers are classified into four groups—classes A, B, C, and D. Research the differences between fire-extinguisher classes, and classify your own.

● Real fire extinguishers use a nozzle on the end of a rubber hose to direct the spray. Design an addition to your experiment to control the direction of the spray.

● Call your city's fire department to find out what chemicals fire extinguishers use to put out fires. Compare the extinguishing process in a real fire extinguisher to this activity in your technology journal.

Notes & Observations

FIRE EXTINGUISHER

Real-World Science and Technology ©1997 Creative Teaching Press

HYDROMETER

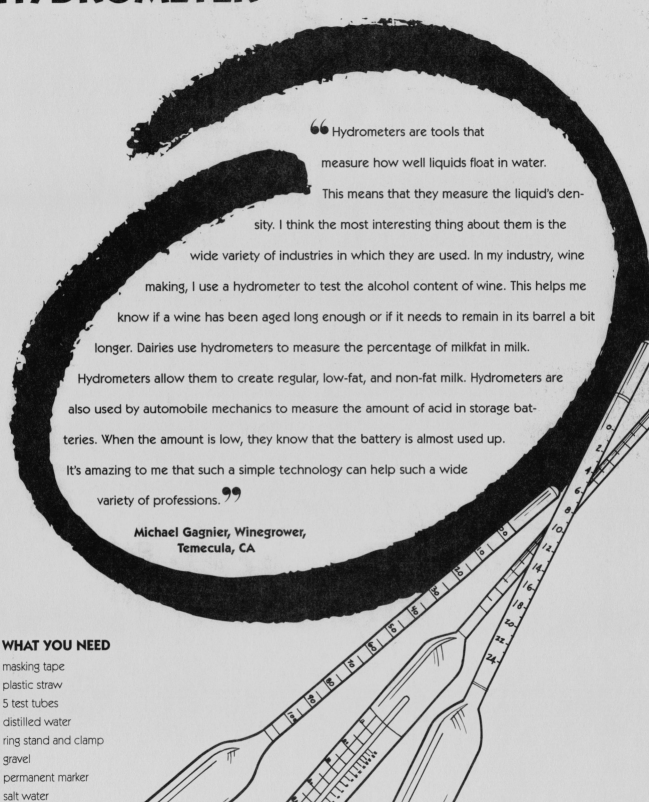

66 Hydrometers are tools that measure how well liquids float in water. This means that they measure the liquid's density. I think the most interesting thing about them is the wide variety of industries in which they are used. In my industry, wine making, I use a hydrometer to test the alcohol content of wine. This helps me know if a wine has been aged long enough or if it needs to remain in its barrel a bit longer. Dairies use hydrometers to measure the percentage of milkfat in milk. Hydrometers allow them to create regular, low-fat, and non-fat milk. Hydrometers are also used by automobile mechanics to measure the amount of acid in storage batteries. When the amount is low, they know that the battery is almost used up. It's amazing to me that such a simple technology can help such a wide variety of professions. 99

**Michael Gagnier, Winegrower,
Temecula, CA**

WHAT YOU NEED

masking tape
plastic straw
5 test tubes
distilled water
ring stand and clamp
gravel
permanent marker
salt water
milk
cooking oil
motor oil

Real-World Science and Technology ©1997 Creative Teaching Press

WHAT YOU DO

1 Fold over the end of the plastic straw and tape it closed.

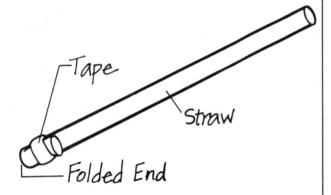

Tape

Straw

Folded End

2 Attach a long strip of masking tape down the length of the straw.

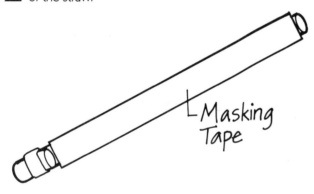

Masking Tape

3 Fill a test tube almost to the top with distilled water. Clamp the test tube to the ring stand.

Distilled Water

4 Place the straw, sealed side first, into the test tube. Drop gravel into the straw until half of the straw has sunk below the water's surface.

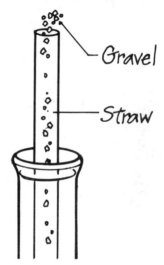

Gravel

Straw

5 Mark the point on the straw even with the water's surface, and remove the straw from the test tube. Write *10* in permanent marker at the mark on the straw. Starting at the top, write *1–9* above the *10*, and *11–20* below at equal intervals.

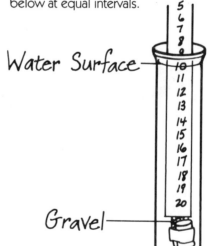

Water Surface

Gravel

6 Fill another test tube with salt water and lower the straw into it. Read the number on the straw even with the surface of the salt water. This is the relative density of salt water. Record this number in your technology journal.

7 Test and record the relative densities of milk, cooking oil, and motor oil.

Real-World Science and Technology ©1997 Creative Teaching Press

HOW IT WORKS

When you make the initial mark on your hydrometer (the straw), you set water's density as the standard for measurement. The density of other liquids is measured relative to water's density. For example, a hydrometer reading of 8 in cooking oil indicates that cooking oil is 0.8 times as dense as water. The hydrometer works because objects float if they are less dense than their surroundings and sink if they are more dense.

STRETCHING TECHNOLOGY

● Design and conduct experiments to find out how temperature affects density.

● Compare results with classmates. Why might there be variances between your results? Create a standardized density scale for your hydrometer.

● What other liquids can you compare using your hydrometer? Create an ordered list of the comparative densities of several liquids.

Notes & Observations

HYDROMETER

HYGROMETER

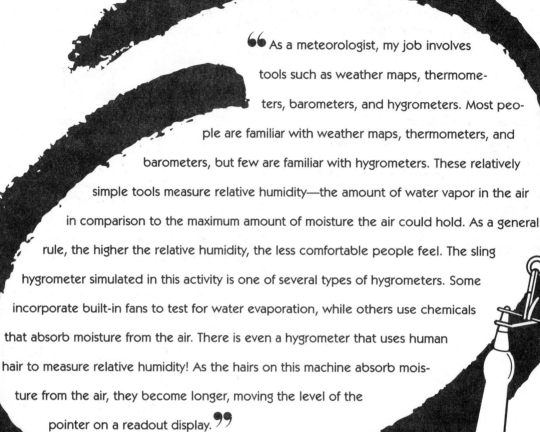

"As a meteorologist, my job involves tools such as weather maps, thermometers, barometers, and hygrometers. Most people are familiar with weather maps, thermometers, and barometers, but few are familiar with hygrometers. These relatively simple tools measure relative humidity—the amount of water vapor in the air in comparison to the maximum amount of moisture the air could hold. As a general rule, the higher the relative humidity, the less comfortable people feel. The sling hygrometer simulated in this activity is one of several types of hygrometers. Some incorporate built-in fans to test for water evaporation, while others use chemicals that absorb moisture from the air. There is even a hygrometer that uses human hair to measure relative humidity! As the hairs on this machine absorb moisture from the air, they become longer, moving the level of the pointer on a readout display."

Karen Daly, Meteorologist

WHAT YOU NEED

2 small paper clips
2 small thermometers
    (backed with metal or plastic)
damp gauze
cellophane tape
plastic straw

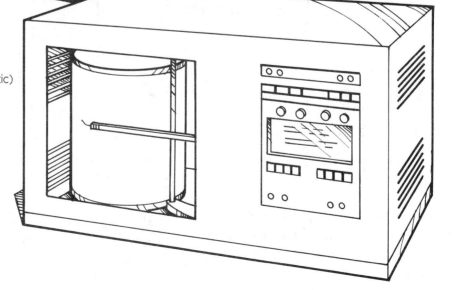

Real-World Science and Technology ©1997 Creative Teaching Press

Real-World Science and Technology ©1997 Creative Teaching Press

1 Bend two paper clips into S shapes. Bend the clips again so the curves form a right angle.

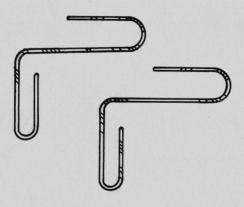

2 Hook a paper clip through the hole in each thermometer's backing. (If the backings do not already have holes, poke them with a pencil or pushpin.)

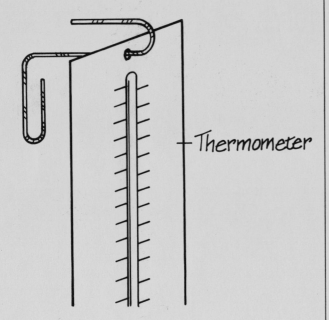

— Thermometer

3 Read and record the temperature on both thermometers. If the temperatures are not the same, set the thermometers next to one another for several minutes, and reread the temperature.

4 Tape several layers of damp gauze around one thermometer's bulb.

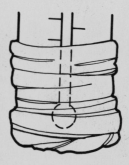

5 Insert the free curve of the paper clips into the same end of the straw. The thermometers should dangle parallel to the straw. Bend the ends of the clips to prevent the thermometers from falling off. (Be sure the paper clips fit snugly into the straw. They may fly out if loose.)

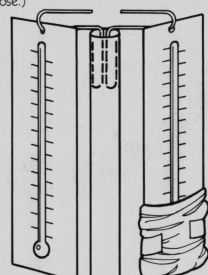

6 Spin the straw for 30 seconds.

7 Record the temperature on both thermometers. (The wet-bulb thermometer should show a lower temperature than the dry-bulb thermometer.)

8 Find the dry-bulb temperature and the wet-bulb temperature on the humidity chart (page 124). Find the intersection of the two lines. This is the percentage of relative humidity.

RELATIVE HUMIDITY CHART

DRY-BULB TEMPERATURES °F

WET-BULB °F	56	58	60	62	64	66	68	70	71	72	73	74	75	76	77	78	79	80	82	84	86	88
38	7																					
40	15	11	7																			
42	25	19	14	9	7																	
44	34	29	22	17	13	8	4															
46	45	38	30	24	18	14	10	6	4	3	1											
48	55	47	40	33	26	21	16	12	10	9	7	5	4	3	1							
50	66	56	48	41	34	29	23	19	17	15	13	11	9	8	6	5	4	3				
52	77	67	57	50	43	36	31	25	23	21	19	17	15	13	12	10	9	7	5	3	1	
54	88	78	68	59	51	44	38	33	30	28	25	23	21	19	17	16	14	12	10	7	5	3
56		89	79	68	60	53	46	40	37	34	32	29	27	25	23	21	19	18	14	12	9	7
58			89	79	70	61	54	48	45	42	39	36	34	31	29	27	25	23	20	16	14	11
60				90	79	71	62	55	52	49	46	43	40	38	35	33	31	29	25	21	18	15
62					90	80	71	64	60	57	53	50	47	44	42	39	37	35	30	26	23	20
64						90	80	72	68	65	61	58	54	51	48	46	43	41	36	32	28	25
66							90	81	77	73	69	65	62	59	56	53	50	47	42	37	33	30
68								90	86	82	78	74	70	66	63	60	57	54	48	43	39	35
70									95	91	86	82	78	74	71	67	64	61	55	49	44	40
72											95	91	86	82	79	75	71	68	61	56	50	46
74													96	91	87	83	79	75	69	62	57	51
76															96	91	87	83	76	69	63	57
78																	96	91	84	76	70	64
80																			92	84	77	70
82																				92	84	77
84																					92	85
86																						92

WET-BULB TEMPERATURES °F

Real-World Science and Technology ©1997 Creative Teaching Press

HOW IT WORKS

Humidity is the amount of water vapor in the air. When humidity is low, sweat evaporates quickly from your body, and your skin feels dry. When humidity is high, sweat cannot evaporate, so your skin feels muggy, sticky, or clammy. Meteorologists use sling hygrometers similar to the one in this activity to measure changes in relative humidity. Water evaporates from the gauze, lowering the temperature of the wet thermometer. The dry thermometer measures the actual temperature of the air. Water evaporates easily in low humidity; therefore, the greater the difference between the two thermometer readings, the lower the humidity. Relative humidity is the amount of moisture in the air compared with the amount of moisture the air could hold if it were saturated at the same temperature.

STRETCHING TECHNOLOGY

● Experiment with the length of time you swing the hygrometer. How does this variable affect your humidity reading?

● Why is the term *relative humidity* used to describe the amount of moisture in the air?

● Measure and record the relative humidity level every day for a month. In your technology journal, create a month-long humidity chart. Try to identify patterns and predict the humidity of coming days.

● Humidity can create problems not only in day-to-day comfort, but in some workplaces as well. Design a way to control humidity levels.

Notes & Observations

HYGROMETER

LASER

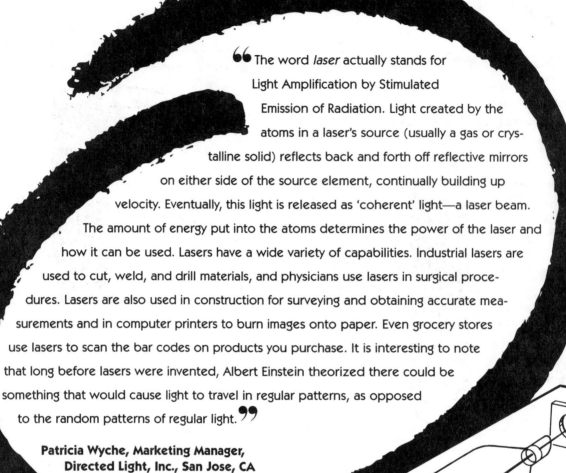

66 The word *laser* actually stands for Light Amplification by Stimulated Emission of Radiation. Light created by the atoms in a laser's source (usually a gas or crystalline solid) reflects back and forth off reflective mirrors on either side of the source element, continually building up velocity. Eventually, this light is released as 'coherent' light—a laser beam. The amount of energy put into the atoms determines the power of the laser and how it can be used. Lasers have a wide variety of capabilities. Industrial lasers are used to cut, weld, and drill materials, and physicians use lasers in surgical procedures. Lasers are also used in construction for surveying and obtaining accurate measurements and in computer printers to burn images onto paper. Even grocery stores use lasers to scan the bar codes on products you purchase. It is interesting to note that long before lasers were invented, Albert Einstein theorized there could be something that would cause light to travel in regular patterns, as opposed to the random patterns of regular light. **99**

**Patricia Wyche, Marketing Manager,
Directed Light, Inc., San Jose, CA**

WHAT YOU NEED

newspaper
scissors
clear plastic bottle
black paint
paintbrush
pushpin
pencil
modeling clay
basin
food coloring
water
flashlight

WHAT YOU DO

CAUTION: Use care when cutting through plastic.

1 Cover the work area with newspaper.

2 Cut off the top 2–3" (5–7.5 cm) of the plastic bottle. Paint one-half of the bottle black (see illustration). Let the paint dry completely.

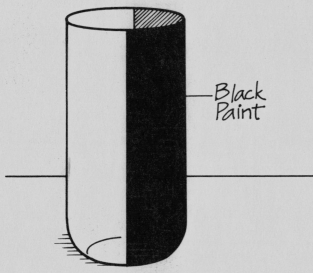

Black Paint

3 Poke the pushpin through the black side of the bottle about 3" (7.5 cm) from the bottom. Widen the hole with the pencil.

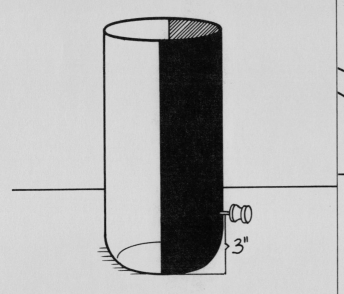

3"

4 Stuff clay into the hole, place the bottle in the basin, and fill the bottle with colored water.

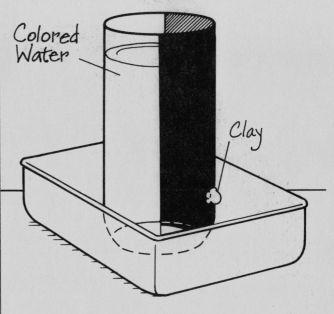

Colored Water

Clay

5 Shine the flashlight at the hole through the unpainted side of the bottle.

6 Turn out the lights in the room, and remove the clay from the hole. Let the water stream land on your fingertip to observe the "laser" (bright stream of light) coming out of the bottle.

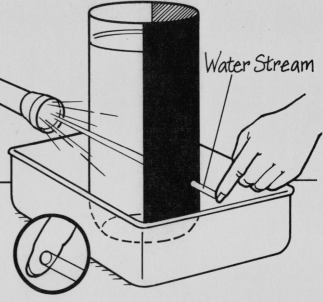

Water Stream

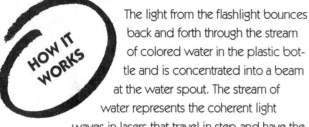

HOW IT WORKS

The light from the flashlight bounces back and forth through the stream of colored water in the plastic bottle and is concentrated into a beam at the water spout. The stream of water represents the coherent light waves in lasers that travel in step and have the same wavelength. In a laser, energy is stored in a solid, liquid, or gas called the *lasing medium.* In a liquid laser, the atoms absorb energy from the electrons moving through the liquid lasing medium and release the energy as light.

STRETCHING TECHNOLOGY

● Real lasers travel much farther and faster than the light in this activity. Redesign your laser to maximize the distance light travels from the bottle. (Hint: Increased pressure will force the stream out faster and farther.)

● Research how a laser's color and source affect its strength and capabilities. Make a chart in your technology journal, including laser types and the careers that use them.

Notes & Observations

LASER

MICROSCOPE

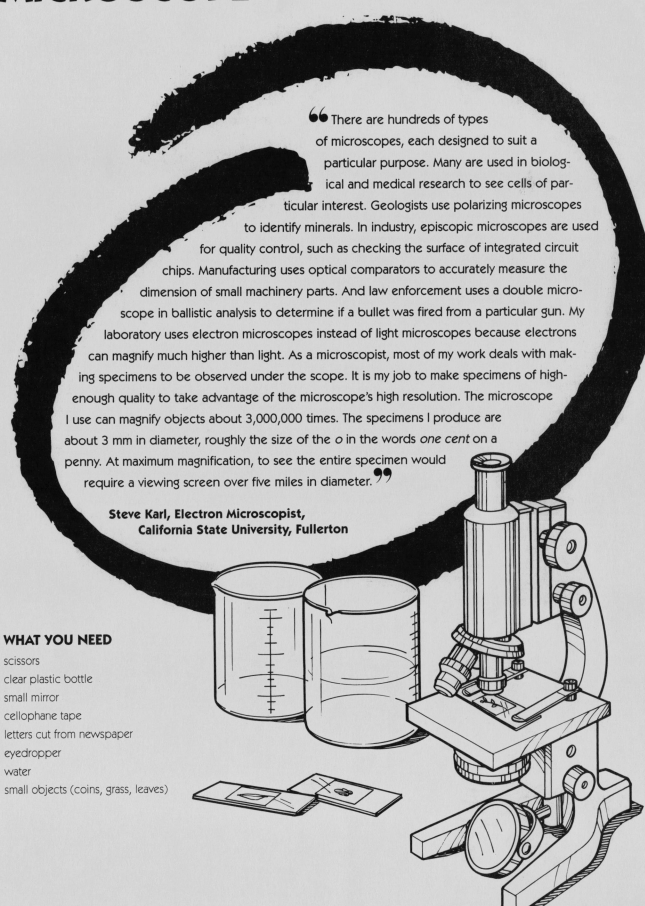

" There are hundreds of types of microscopes, each designed to suit a particular purpose. Many are used in biological and medical research to see cells of particular interest. Geologists use polarizing microscopes to identify minerals. In industry, episcopic microscopes are used for quality control, such as checking the surface of integrated circuit chips. Manufacturing uses optical comparators to accurately measure the dimension of small machinery parts. And law enforcement uses a double microscope in ballistic analysis to determine if a bullet was fired from a particular gun. My laboratory uses electron microscopes instead of light microscopes because electrons can magnify much higher than light. As a microscopist, most of my work deals with making specimens to be observed under the scope. It is my job to make specimens of high-enough quality to take advantage of the microscope's high resolution. The microscope I use can magnify objects about 3,000,000 times. The specimens I produce are about 3 mm in diameter, roughly the size of the *o* in the words *one cent* on a penny. At maximum magnification, to see the entire specimen would require a viewing screen over five miles in diameter. **"**

**Steve Karl, Electron Microscopist,
California State University, Fullerton**

WHAT YOU NEED

scissors
clear plastic bottle
small mirror
cellophane tape
letters cut from newspaper
eyedropper
water
small objects (coins, grass, leaves)

WHAT YOU DO

CAUTION: Use care when cutting through plastic.

1 Cut the top off the plastic bottle. From opposite sides, cut strips 2" (5 cm) wide and 6" (15 cm) long. Flatten the strips as much as possible. Set them aside.

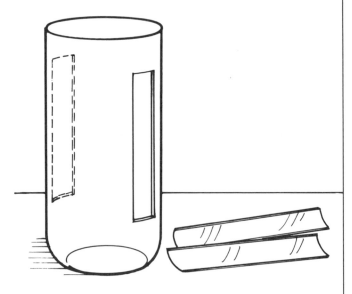

2 Place the mirror, reflective side up, in the bottom of the bottle.

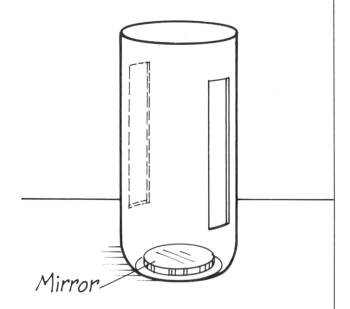

Mirror

3 Wedge one strip horizontally through the tops of the slits in the bottle. Tape it in place.

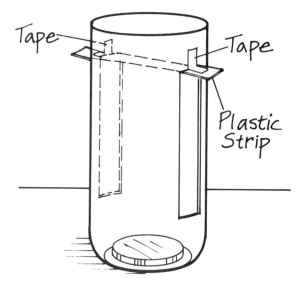

Tape • Tape • Plastic Strip

4 Place a letter cut from newspaper in the center of the other strip. Insert it through the bottoms of the slits. Center a drop of water on the top strip. Keep the bottle very still to prevent the water drop from spreading out or spilling off the strip.

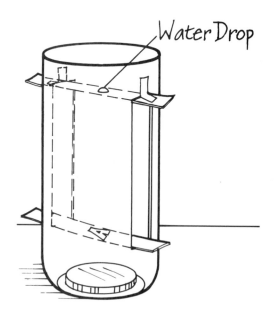

Water Drop

5 Look at the letter through the drop of water. Place other small objects on the "slide" and observe them through the water drop.

Real-World Science and Technology ©1997 Creative Teaching Press

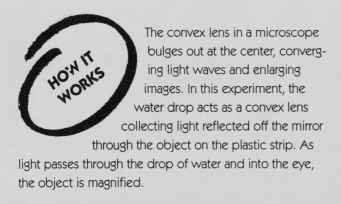

HOW IT WORKS

The convex lens in a microscope bulges out at the center, converging light waves and enlarging images. In this experiment, the water drop acts as a convex lens collecting light reflected off the mirror through the object on the plastic strip. As light passes through the drop of water and into the eye, the object is magnified.

STRETCHING TECHNOLOGY

● Investigate ways to make the microscope enlarge images even more. Write a description of your methods in your technology journal.

● Look at specimens under the hand-made microscope and a magnifying glass. Do the objects look the same? How are they different?

● In your journal, list careers that use microscopes and describe how they use them.

Notes & Observations

MICROSCOPE

MOTION PICTURES

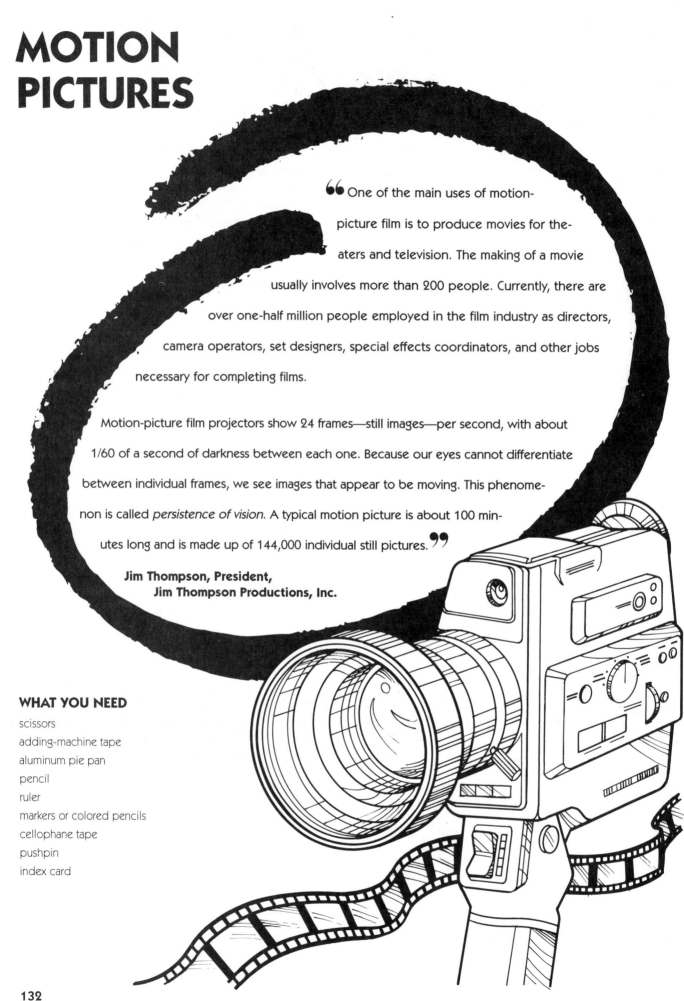

❝One of the main uses of motion-picture film is to produce movies for theaters and television. The making of a movie usually involves more than 200 people. Currently, there are over one-half million people employed in the film industry as directors, camera operators, set designers, special effects coordinators, and other jobs necessary for completing films.

Motion-picture film projectors show 24 frames—still images—per second, with about 1/60 of a second of darkness between each one. Because our eyes cannot differentiate between individual frames, we see images that appear to be moving. This phenomenon is called *persistence of vision*. A typical motion picture is about 100 minutes long and is made up of 144,000 individual still pictures.❞

**Jim Thompson, President,
Jim Thompson Productions, Inc.**

WHAT YOU NEED

scissors
adding-machine tape
aluminum pie pan
pencil
ruler
markers or colored pencils
cellophane tape
pushpin
index card

CAUTION: Poke holes away from your body.

1 Cut a strip of adding-machine tape long enough to fit securely around the edge of an aluminum pie pan.

2 Divide the strip into 20 equal sections with a pencil and ruler. Make the lines barely visible.

3 In one section (frame), draw a simple cartoon figure beginning to walk, run, or jump. Repeat the drawing in the following sections, changing features slightly to give a sense of movement.

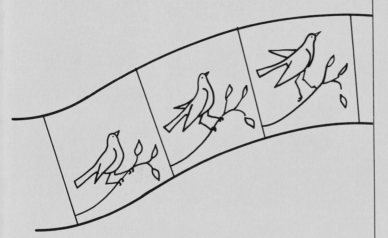

4 Color your "frames" with brightly-colored markers or pencils.

5 Tape the "filmstrip" along the edge of the pie pan.

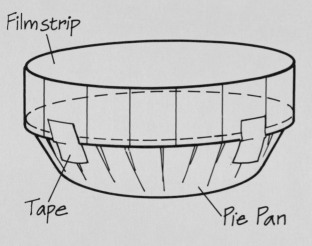

Filmstrip

Tape

Pie Pan

6 Poke a pinhole through the center of the pan. Push the pencil through the hole until about 5" (12.5 cm) stick out of the bottom. This is the "spinner."

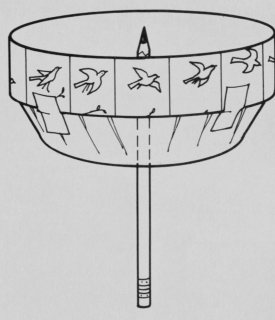

7 Poke a pinhole through an index card. Close one eye and look at the "movie" through the pinhole as you spin the pencil.

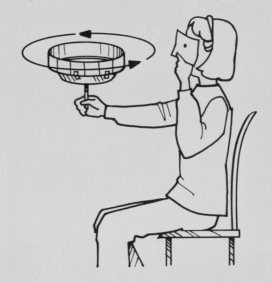

A moving picture shows 24 frames per second. At this speed, your eyes cannot distinguish one still picture from another, and you see them as a continuously changing, single image. The picture seems to flow smoothly because your eyes blend individual frames into one another (persistence of vision). The picture seems to be moving because each image is slightly different, hence the name "motion picture." In this activity, rapid spinning of your "movie" prevents your eye from distinguishing individual images, causing persistence of vision.

● Make a flip book by cutting 20–30 small rectangular pieces of white paper and stapling them together like a book. Draw and color a figure that changes slightly from page to page. Show a person crying, the sun rising and setting, or a clown popping out of a box. View your flip-book movie by holding the book by the staples and quickly flipping through it.

● Draw half of an image on a cardboard square and the other half on another square. Tape the two drawings together, back to back, on opposite sides of a pencil. Spin the pictures by rolling the pencil between your hands. In your technology journal, explain how persistence of vision applies to this toy—called a *thaumatrope*—and compare it to your movie.

Notes & Observations

MOTION PICTURES

SLIDE PROJECTOR

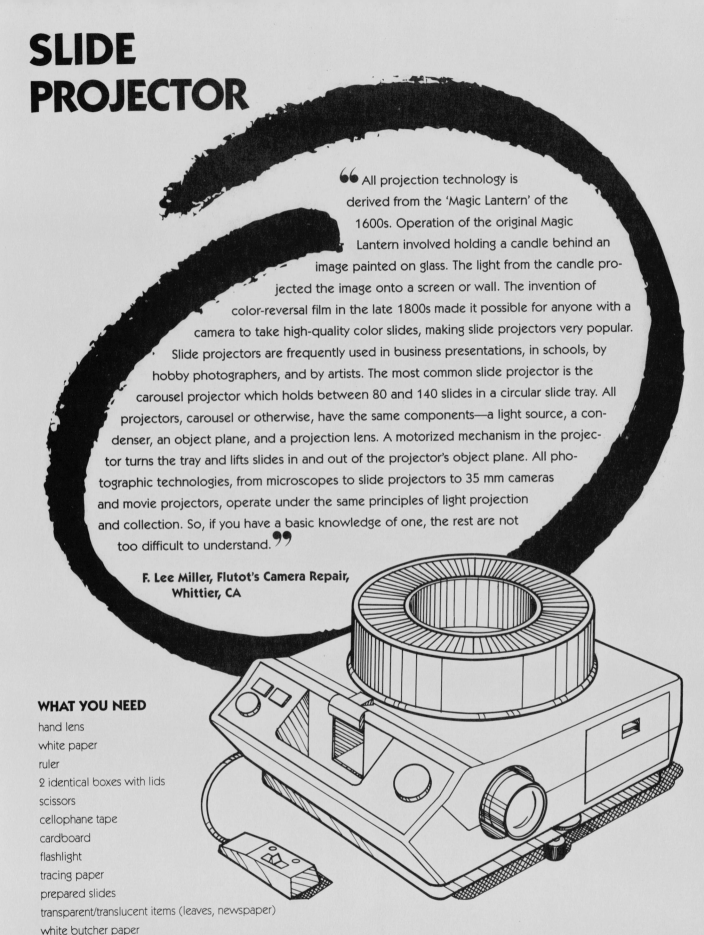

> 66 All projection technology is derived from the 'Magic Lantern' of the 1600s. Operation of the original Magic Lantern involved holding a candle behind an image painted on glass. The light from the candle projected the image onto a screen or wall. The invention of color-reversal film in the late 1800s made it possible for anyone with a camera to take high-quality color slides, making slide projectors very popular. Slide projectors are frequently used in business presentations, in schools, by hobby photographers, and by artists. The most common slide projector is the carousel projector which holds between 80 and 140 slides in a circular slide tray. All projectors, carousel or otherwise, have the same components—a light source, a condenser, an object plane, and a projection lens. A motorized mechanism in the projector turns the tray and lifts slides in and out of the projector's object plane. All photographic technologies, from microscopes to slide projectors to 35 mm cameras and movie projectors, operate under the same principles of light projection and collection. So, if you have a basic knowledge of one, the rest are not too difficult to understand. 99

F. Lee Miller, Flutot's Camera Repair, Whittier, CA

WHAT YOU NEED

hand lens
white paper
ruler
2 identical boxes with lids
scissors
cellophane tape
cardboard
flashlight
tracing paper
prepared slides
transparent/translucent items (leaves, newspaper)
white butcher paper

Real-World Science and Technology © 1997 Creative Teaching Press

CAUTION: Use care when cutting through cardboard.

1 Focus light through the lens on white paper. Measure the distance between the lens and the paper when you get a sharp image of the light source. This distance measures the focal point of the lens.

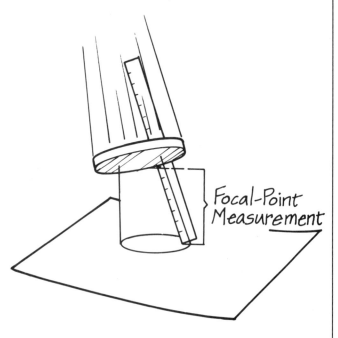

Focal-Point Measurement

2 Cut off the top of one box so its height is equal to the focal-point measurement from step 1.

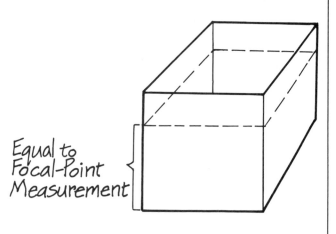

Equal to Focal-Point Measurement

3 Find and mark the center of the box lid and the box bottom. Center the hand lens over each mark and trace around it. Cut out both shapes, and tape the lens securely to the hole in the box lid. The hole in the box bottom should align with the hole in the lid. Tape the lid on top of the box.

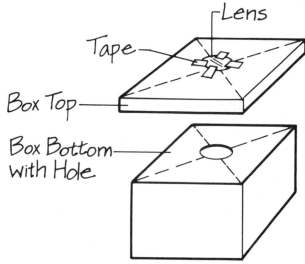

Lens

Tape

Box Top

Box Bottom with Hole

4 Cut out a cardboard rectangle slightly narrower and longer than the box bottom.

5 Cut a square the size of a projection slide [approximately 2" x 2" (5 cm x 5 cm)] in the center of the cardboard. This is your slide holder.

Cardboard

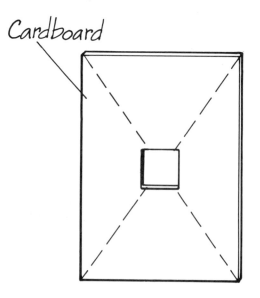

Real-World Science and Technology ©1997 Creative Teaching Press

6 Make a hole in the bottom of the second box the same size as the hole in the first box.

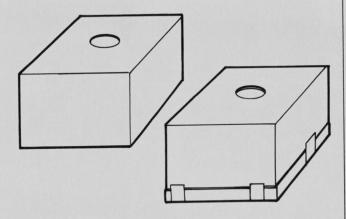

7 Place the boxes bottom to bottom, aligning the holes. Tape the boxes together, leaving a small space between to insert the slide holder.

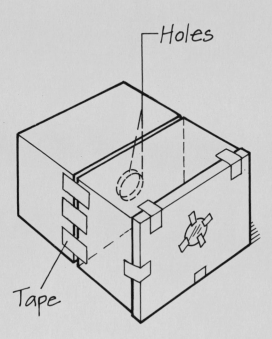

Holes

Tape

8 Cover the flashlight with tracing paper to dampen and more evenly distribute the light. Place the flashlight (turned on) in the second box. Align the flashlight with the holes in the box bottoms and the lens, and replace the lid.

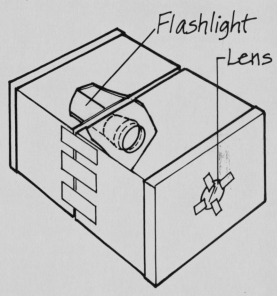

Flashlight

Lens

9 Tape the object to be projected (prepared slide, transparent/translucent object) to the slide holder, turn the holder upside down, and insert it in the slot between the two boxes.

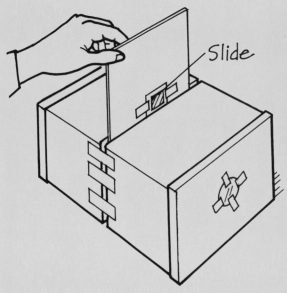

Slide

10 Darken the room and aim the projector at a movie screen or white butcher paper taped to a wall.

Your projector functions much like a real slide projector. An image is projected through an adjustable lens which focuses the image for a sharp, clear picture. The larger the lens, the brighter the picture. The slide holder holds the transparent slide as in a carousel projector. The light source in the back diffuses the light so it passes evenly through all of the slide. Slides are inserted upside down because the projector inverts images much like the human eye.

STRETCHING TECHNOLOGY

● Design a way to adjust the focus of your slide projector.

● Compare a simple magnifying glass to your slide projector. List similarities and differences in your technology journal.

● Create new slides to project. Experiment with various colors on materials such as tracing paper, cellophane, and transparent acetate. Which colors and materials work best?

Notes & Observations

SLIDE PROJECTOR

Real-World Science and Technology ©1997 Creative Teaching Press

SOLAR
WATER
HEATER

66 Although they are not prac-

tical in some areas, solar water heaters are

an inexpensive, efficient appliance in hot,

sunny places. Because they do not consume fuel, like gas and

electric water heaters, the monthly cost of maintaining a solar water

heater is relatively low. Also, solar water heaters are more helpful to the environ-

ment for many reasons. They do not create any polluting waste products, and they

do not draw from non-renewable fuel sources such as coal, oil, or natural gas.

Unfortunately, because they are dependent on consistent sunlight, solar water

heaters may not be as reliable as other water heaters. However, their insulated

tanks do store enough hot water to last through some rather lengthy dark

or sunless periods. 99

**Juan Benicio,
Solar Water Heating Sales Representative**

WHAT YOU NEED

12" x 18" (30 cm x 45 cm) box
black construction paper
black spray paint
8' (2.5 m) clear flexible tube
　　[1 1/2–2" (4–5 cm)-diameter]
scissors
electrical tape
plate glass (slightly larger than box)
books
2 pails
water
clothespin
2 thermometers

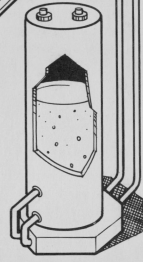

Real-World Science and Technology ©1997 Creative Teaching Press

WHAT YOU DO

1 Line the inside of the box with black construction paper.

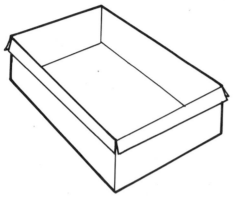

2 Spray-paint the flexible tube black, and let it dry.

3 At opposite ends of one side of the box, cut two holes large enough to fit the tube.

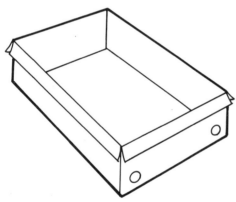

4 Run the tube through the first hole, curve it into S-shaped coils inside the box, and run it out the second hole. Use electrical tape to secure the tube to the box.

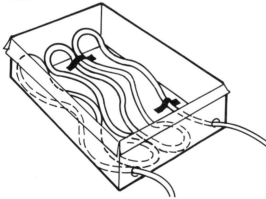

5 Cover the box with the glass. Set the apparatus on a stack of books in direct sunlight.

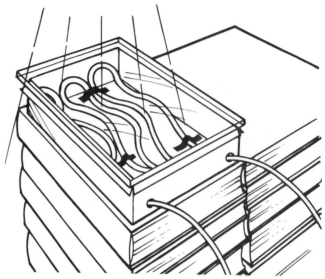

6 Fill one pail with water, place it next to the solar heater, and drop one end of the tube inside. Place the other pail below the solar heater so the other end of the tube hangs over it.

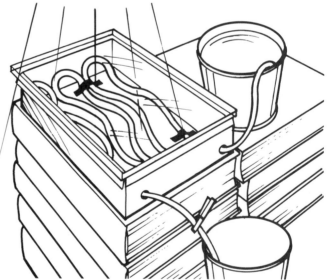

7 Suck gently on the tube hanging over the empty pail to create a siphoning action. Clamp the tube with a clothespin so the water comes through slowly.

8 Place a thermometer in each pail. Observe and record the differences in water temperature in each pail at one-minute intervals in your technology journal.

Real-World Science and Technology ©1997 Creative Teaching Press